SuperScout

SuperScout

Thirty-five Years of Major League Scouting

Jim Russo
with
Bob Hammel

Bonus Books, Inc., Chicago

96 95 94 93 92   5 4 3 2 1

Library of Congress Catalog Card Number: 91-77021

International Standard Book Number: 0-929387-69-4

Bonus Books, Inc.
160 East Illinois Street
Chicago, Illinois 60611

First Edition

Printed in the United States of America

Composition by Point West, Inc., Carol Stream, Illinois

To Betty's Memory

Also to my children. Steve and Susan Wrenkle, Cliff and Lisa Russo, Bryan and Jennifer Baehr, Dan and Nancy Blakeley, and Ron. Also a special thanks to Norma for her advice and support.

Contents

Acknowledgments

I owe a debt of gratitude to so many for their advice, encouragement, and help.

Tony Robello my benefactor, to Mary Buchheit, Zack Cook, Don and Mick King, Roger and Pat Groves, Merle and Judy Heinlein, Jerry and Laurel, Gail and Ann Noble, Vera Russo, Ralph and Margaret Noll.

To Bob Brown and Helen Conklin of the Oriole front office, and Arthur Richman of the Yankees and Browns.

Former *Sporting News* writer and editor Cliff and Evelyn Kachline. Indiana University broadcasters Don Fischer and Chuck Marlowe. And to Tim Garl and Kit Klingehoffer.

The great writer of the *St. Louis Post-Dispatch* Bob Broeg.

To Paul and Marian Blakeley, Charlie and Alice Chambers, Harlan and Joy Dotson, Ernie and Bobette Janus, Tom Dewey, Angela Esquivel, Chuck Fattore, Dan and Chris Gray, Al Grosch, Bob Lallinger, Henry and Phyllis Diederich, Irv Knueppe.

Also to Bill Madden, Greg Riddoch, Bucky Dent, and Tony Kubek who have always championed the importance of the scouts to a ballclub.

My special appreciation to my agent Tom Connor, and to my editor Larry Razbadouski. Also to all the ballclubs and others who supplied pictures for this endeavor.

1

Flying High with the Birds

All around me was Dodger blue. And I saw brown, St. Louis Brown. Through tears.

There is no question at all about my moment of baseball moments: Opening day. Of the 1966 World Series. Baseball's sixty-third but my first, with direct involvement.

Sure I cried. You have to understand, the World Series is baseball's improvement on heaven; you don't have to die to get there. If necessary, I would have considered it, as would some greats of the game whose first Series hasn't, or will not ever, come—Don Mattingly and Dale Murphy from today's generation, Ernie Banks from yesterday's, Luke Appling from the one before. That's where heaven has its edge. Absolute saints of the sport of baseball can't get in a World Series on their own. It takes a team.

Just how special a moment it was certainly was in my mind on the fifth of October, 1966, when the Baltimore Orioles were out there on the glitziest field of the other league. They made the introductions, and played the national anthem, and it hit me, in the heart, in the throat, in suddenly watery eyes:

"I can't believe it. We really are here. In the World Series."

If you don't shed a tear at a moment like that, I don't think you're human.

I was human at every World Series the Orioles made.

Especially my first time. That first day I knew what Lou Gehrig had meant—and I knew that he truly did *mean* it—when he stood at the plate in Yankee Stadium on the Fourth of July in 1939, his record streak of 2,130 games played forced to an end by pain from the terrible illness that caused his death, and told the 61,808 who had come to honor him: ''I'm the luckiest man on the face of the earth.''

Anyone ever privileged to spend a lifetime in baseball has had that feeling, or should have had. Joe DiMaggio's autobiography was entitled, *Lucky to Be a Yankee*. That day in 1966, Jim Russo felt lucky to be an American, because America created and nurtured and cherished this game that was my life...and luckiest of all to be an Oriole, because we had made those Yankees with their Ruth-Gehrig-DiMaggio-Mantle tradition our working model, overtaken them for at least this precious day, and replaced them in the role that had seemed to be their birthright: the American League team in the World Series.

Now, we wanted to act like those Yankees.

And never very far back in my mind was that wry realization that gave it all such dimension:

We were the old St. Louis Browns.

Don't get me wrong: I had felt lucky—hey, I *was* lucky—to be a Brown. But I felt a hell of a lot luckier to be an Oriole.

I felt that way even though I was the Oriole with his chin stuck out.

We were changing history that year, and I was part of it. For the last few weeks of the season, I had traveled with the Dodgers specifically to get scouting information that we put to work in the Series. That's standard now, but then it had never been done before. I can't honestly say never. In 1929, Connie Mack of the Philadelphia Athletics had an old, sore-armed pitcher named Howard Ehmke who needed the rest anyway, so Mr. Mack had him spend the last three weeks of the season watching the Cubs.

Ehmke was thirty-five, a journeyman at best (166-166 lifetime). He pitched only ten innings the next year and retired—the classic player at the end of the trail. He was on a staff with six other guys who won more games than he did that season, including the immortal, Lefty Grove. But Connie Mack opened the World Series with junk-baller Ehmke.

And he won. Hall of Famers Rogers Hornsby (.380, 39 homers, 149 RBI that year) and Hack Wilson (.345, 39, 159) each went 0-for-4 and struck out twice, and Ehmke, who had only 20 strikeouts that whole season, set a World Series strikeout record (13) that stood for twenty-four years.

Do you suppose somebody should have caught on way back then that there was something to scouting?

Successful as it was on that first trial, though, nobody else tried advance scouting of the other league prior to a Series. I'd have to think one reason for that is baseball conservatism and superstition, the kind of thing that makes it a sin to talk about a no-hitter in progress. In a sense, the team sending its scout out to look at the other league was Red Auerbach lighting a cigar: "This pennant is won, let's look beyond."

I'll assure you we weren't doing that. In 1966, our franchise hadn't won a pennant in twenty-two years and the Baltimore Orioles—our Baltimore Orioles, anyway, not the prehistoric ones with Wee Willie Keeler and John McGraw and Wilbert Robinson—had never won one. Humility was not a problem on our club in 1966.

We just believed that if there was a chance that we could be in the World Series, we wanted to give it our best shot.

And I was the guy designated to get us ready to take that shot.

I stayed with the Dodgers for twenty-two games, and there I've got to give our general manager, Harry Dalton, a lot of credit. The Dodgers were third in their league at the time—the first week in September—but Harry was the one who said if we were going to do this scouting thing, we should forget the Giants and Pirates ahead of them and go with the Dodgers because their pitching was going to win. I felt the same way, and nothing

I saw traveling with them changed my mind. I saw them go 12-2 over one stretch, including four straight shutouts against the Astros.

I'll tell you how novel the situation was: on road trips during that stretch, I flew with the Dodgers on their private airplane. Walter Alston, their manager, invited me.

Al Kubski, our West Coast scout, and Harry Craft, our Texas scout, joined me for the last few games. I spent fourteen hours writing all the notes out on a legal pad, and when it was typed, it came out to sixteen single-spaced pages—too much, but, remember, it *was* my first World Series report.

The Dodgers were the standards of the day then. They had won world championships in 1963 and 1965, sweeping the Yankees in 1963. They were the team with Sandy Koufax and Don Drysdale—a whole lot more, too, including a hell of a weapon in Walter Alston himself. But in the 1960s when you thought of baseball superiority you thought of the Dodgers and of Koufax and Drysdale: the one (left-hander Koufax) simply the best pitcher I had ever seen, the other (right-hander Drysdale) maybe the meanest.

My job in those last twenty-two games was to find a way to beat them. "Mission Impossible" was big on TV then. It always started with the hero of the show listening to a tape recording: "Your assignment, if you choose to accept it, Mr. Phelps, is to . . ." I was Mr. Phelps, and as I sat in the stands that bright October afternoon in classy, haughty, imposing Dodger Stadium, I wasn't too sure that both I and my ballclub had not taken on an impossible mission.

I sure didn't let any of that get into the report I put together, and the ballclub distributed to each of our players to be read on the flight to Los Angeles for the Series.

Koufax had just closed out maybe the best four-year run any pitcher ever had, certainly any pitcher I had ever watched: 25-5 in 1963, 1.88 ERA, two complete-game victories over the Yankees in the World Series; 19-5 with a 1.74 ERA in 1964, when he missed a big part of the season with a tender arm; 26-8 and 2.04 in 1965, with two more Series victories—both of them shutouts against a powerhouse offense, the Minnesota Twins; 27-9 and a 1.73 ERA, with a career-high 317 strikeouts, in this season, 1966.

And what our guys read from me on Koufax was:

"Has been a *great* pitcher but would call him a *good* pitcher now..."

I look at that now and I think, "Jesus Christ, Russo, I know you hate to use the word 'great' for anybody, but calling this guy 'good'...?"

But that was the tone for the whole section on Koufax—impressed but not awed, a description of a man formidable but beatable.

"Standard assortment: Fastball, curve ball, change-up... Overhand delivery...Fastball is a *two*..."

This, of course, was on a rating system with one representing the very best. Pray tell, you may be wondering, who had a one if Sandy Koufax' fastball was a two?

Let me try to explain my rating: I thought Koufax was a great pitcher, but I felt he had lost just a shade off his velocity. But just a little bit...and if Sandy Koufax loses a little, he's still got a hell of a lot.

I just didn't want to mislead our guys and tell them I thought he still had as good a fastball as he had ever had. And maybe there was a little bit of subtle positive reinforcement at work there, too. All of us in baseball pretty much had Koufax built up as unbeatable, not without cause. If there was a theme of the entire scouting report, it came in two editorial comments I slipped into the accumulation of data:

"Let's not panic against this club."

And, as my conclusion:

"We can beat this club."

Back to that pseudo-two fastball of Koufax:

"Rises rather than sinks. Hitters have been helping him much too often, swinging at high strikes and at balls out of strike zone. *Try to stay away from his high fastball that is above the strike zone*...

"Curve ball is big-breaking type. Now lacks its former velocity and sharpness. Still has a sharp-breaking curve but has not thrown this pitch for strikes...His big breaking curve has been hanging, and this is why he has stayed with the fastball...

"Throws straight change occasionally against the better hitters but not often. Usually sticks with hard stuff...In the last three innings in a 4-0 game with Houston, threw only two curves. Faced thirty-four hitters; started only five with curves. Last game pitched: 100 fastballs (69 strikes, 31 balls), 25 curves (15 strikes), 4 changes (2 strikes)...

"Could be bunted on...

"Has to throw with long throwing motion. Below-average move to first. Because of big windup, would try to steal on him. Doesn't throw often to first base; would steal on first movement and go regardless of the count."

And on Drysdale, 23-12 the year before but just 13-16 in 1966:

"Not the effective pitcher of former years, but don't sell him short in an important game...Has two bad knees. Little clumsy getting off the mound. Once failed to cover first base on ground ball to first baseman. Would bunt on him...Faced thirty-one hitters, started only six out with breaking pitches...On two-strike count, doesn't waste pitch very often...Average fastball (3-plus)...Average slider (3-plus), fairly quick and somewhat flat. Gets hurt when it is up...Slider is his second-best pitch. Curve is not a good pitch for him...Summary: Has been somewhat ineffective this year. Must pitch low to be effective."

Almost as an afterthought on Drysdale:

"Will knock batters down. Good competitor..."

I think I put that in there so the former National Leaguers on our team would know I actually had spent all that time watching the right club.

And Game 1 began.

The Dodgers had been forced to use Koufax on the final day of the season to win the pennant, so Drysdale was their pitcher. Luis Aparicio, one of the few players we had on our club who had been in a Series before, battled Drysdale well but flied to right. Russ Snyder walked.

Frank Robinson came up.

The World Series wasn't five minutes old and already it was mano a mano, our toughest and meanest hitter against their toughest and meanest pitcher. Frank Robinson didn't need any notes from Jim Russo to know all about Don Drysdale. Robinson knew Drysdale would put him on his back without the slightest pang of conscience—knew it because Drysdale had done it who knows how many times when they had faced each other in Robinson's ten seasons with the Cincinnati Reds, the same years that were Drysdale's first ten as a Dodger. And Drysdale knew that knocking Robinson down, sweet as it probably felt for him at the time, wasn't the best thing in the world to do because the Robinson who got back up leaned over the plate just as menacingly and swung maybe even a little bit harder and better than the one who was knocked down.

Drysdale threw...

Robinson swung...

And Jim Russo almost lost it right there.

Home run.

What a beautiful, wonderful arrival for the Baltimore Orioles in the World Series.

And now it was Brooks Robinson's turn, the first time at bat in a World Series for the consummate Oriole: signed into our system right out of high school in Little Rock, Arkansas; brought along, quickly but carefully; exposed to the majors when neither he nor our club was really capable of competing but a superb player and competitor and leader now, his professionalism too deep and too pure to permit the tiniest bit of resentment to surface at the way another man, another Robinson even, had come along to upstage him when the Orioles finally broke through.

Drysdale threw...

Robinson swung...

Hell, even the spot in the left-field stands where the ball landed was almost the same. America had just sat down to get acquainted with this new October ballclub and the Orioles were up 3-0 on the Dodgers and Don Drysdale.

Baseball creates more cliches than anything with the possible exception of war. Leadership is a cliche word in both. The Lord never put me on a battlefield, but when the day comes that I go up there to see Him, I know damned well that I'll still be able to say that I never saw leadership spelled out, defined and put on display better than the way the two Robinsons did for the Baltimore Orioles in that stunning two minutes of that epochal afternoon in Dodger Stadium, October 5, 1966.

I've always ranked among the most courageous things I've ever been privileged to witness the simple act of our fifth hitter, Boog Powell, stepping into the box right after the two Robinsons' home runs. Every baseball fan in America knew how super-competitor Drysdale had to be seething at that very instant, and the biggest target in baseball—all 6-foot-5, 230-going-on-250 pounds of him—was standing up there like a carnival kewpie doll.

I can't honestly tell you what happened. The record book says Boog popped out to third, and somewhere Boog's relatives and his insurance man, and maybe even Boog himself, must have wiped their brows in relief.

All I know is that the Birds were on the wing for the most glorious flight of my life, a flight that lasted twenty years and carried me into my baseball afterlife feeling two things, lucky and blessed.

Lucky to have spent a working lifetime in a game I loved but couldn't really play.

Blessed to have done it with Baltimore, for reasons I want you to hear.

2

A Fan-tastic Life

*I love this game. As a boy I was a baseball fan, and as an old, re-
tired "boy" I am still a fan. And as a scout I was a fan, until I
accepted the fact that my judgments, if wrong, could cost my club
millions of dollars—and, if right, could make my club millions of
dollars. Then I realized that for me it was a business.*

All of us grew up with the idea that any man could be president of the United States. I love my country as much as anyone,
but that stuff is ridiculous. Anyone who is male and white and
rich and well connected and saleable on TV has a chance, but
that leaves out about 99.99 percent of Americans.

But I offer myself as evidence that any man—and, with the
Pam Postema umpiring attempt and rejection still a fresh memory, I probably have to keep it male—any man *can* make it in
baseball. My lifetime in it came only because I loved the game
enough to work hard and maximize the very few God-given
baseball gifts I had.

I do not understate. There was nothing about my heritage
to suggest I should have a chance to live the life I have. Lord

knows I wasn't a player, and I wasn't from a baseball area. I grew up in a town that didn't even have a minor league team within 100 miles, let alone a major league team, and never has had a big league player—Huntington, Indiana. Mention of Huntington gives that opening reference to the presidency a little humor because, yes, another who calls it home is Vice President Dan Quayle. His surprise selection as a running mate by George Bush, and his election, gave our town a little more fame than I ever did, and Dan Quayle from that little town of 15,000 or so obviously could be president—which doesn't particularly refute my statement. Dan is male and white and rich and well connected and still has a chance to overcome the enormously negative start he got and be TV-saleable, because he is handsome and a whole lot smarter than his ridiculers want to believe. (I have to rely on friends for that assessment. I've never met Dan, though I would love to. I left Huntington just about the time he was born. And a very, very prized place on my living room wall carries a framed invitation my wife and I had to the John F. Kennedy Inauguration, which says a little bit about political differences between the Quayles and the Russos.)

My love for the game developed as a radio fan, listening to Bob Elson, Pat Flanigan, Jack Brickhouse, all those Chicago announcers. I was a Pittsburgh Pirates fan, because my brother Tony told me they were a good team. And they were good, with the Waners and Arky Vaughan, just good enough to break my heart.

I can remember shedding tears, honest to God, the day Gabby Hartnett hit the "homer in the gloaming" at Wrigley Field off Mace Brown of the Pirates in a key victory for the Cubs in 1938. I was listening. I had sprinted out of school that day, hoping to get downtown to the newsstand where they always had the game broadcast going. I got there, out of breath, just in time to hear that damned crack of the bat and feel my Pirates die. (I later became a real good friend of Mace Brown, who was a scout for the Red Sox—a really nice man, but that thing with Hartnett was not something he wanted to talk about. Another pitcher on that Pittsburgh team, Joe Bowman, became a scout for us, and I asked him once: "Joe, what the hell did he throw to Hartnett?" It was about forty years later, and he was a good friend of Mace's, too, but he still flared up a little: "He threw a *breaking* ball. Can you believe that? It was getting dark, and Mace could pop the ball pretty well, but the son of a bitch didn't throw a fastball, he threw a breaking ball.")

I got my start in baseball by getting some friends together to form a team and play on weekends. I was seventeen, but I was the manager, because I was the guy who sent a letter to the *Fort Wayne Journal-Gazette* to advertise for teams willing to play and made up a schedule. When I came back from World War II, I got a team together again and we weren't bad. The St. Louis Browns had a scout in the area, P.L. McCormick, who signed one of the smartest pitchers I've ever seen—Ned Garver, from Ney, Ohio. Until Steve Carlton won 27 games for the Phillies in 1972, Garver (20-12 for the Browns in 1951) was the last pitcher to win 20 games for a last-place team, that's how good he was. McCormick signed two of my players, too, a pitcher named Arden Schenkel (cousin of the great TV announcer who also was from Huntington County, Chris Schenkel) and a catcher named Max Risser. Neither one made it to the majors—I believe Schenkel could have, but his arm went bad. Still, just having two guys sign pro contracts showed that our team wasn't too bad. That meant a lot to me, but so did the link their signings gave me with someone actually connected with organized baseball: McCormick.

At that point, though, I wasn't even dreaming about a baseball career. Like most returned GIs, I was a little bit adrift about what I wanted to do. So, I reached for the stars. I thought it would be the best life in the world to sit there like Bob Elson and watch a ballgame and tell people what was going on. I went to Huntington College for a year and took a special radio broadcasting course at Indiana University-Fort Wayne. Then I went to a radio school in Chicago, Columbia College, where my live broadcasting experience consisted of covering teams from Hines Military Hospital. The only listeners were the patients, but it was good experience. It got me a job in Alma, Michigan, doing Alma College football and basketball games and high school basketball games.

I also kept in contact with P.L. McCormick, and he helped me become a "commission scout" with the Browns. Commission scout meant I had no salary and no power, but if I recommended a player that they signed and kept, I made money with each step he made up the minor league ladder—about $100 each time, which was enough to keep you interested. If he made the big league club, it was $1,000, and that wasn't bad.

I'll never forget my first signing. It's hard to forget a name like Vachel Perkins.

Vachel was a really good, hard-throwing pitcher for a high school team in Edmore, Michigan, which was near Alma. He was good enough that a lot of clubs were starting to move in on him, but I got him for the Browns—with their permission, of course, but nobody else from the club saw him but me. His father, Herbert, had a big potato farm, and the first time I met him, he was out in the middle of a field, cultivating those potatoes. I climbed over a fence, walked through the field, introduced myself and started trying to sell the Browns. I kind of surprised him. He told me, "The other scouts come to the edge of the field and wait for me to come to them. You're the only one who came out to me." I told him, "Herbert, I'd walk across a field of horseshit to talk to you." He loved that.

I would have, too, because Vachel was good. He won 24 games one year, most of anyone in the whole Browns organization, at Pine Bluff in the Cotton States League. I almost got that $1,000. He had a good year at San Antonio in Double-A—which was as high as the Browns had a team then, that's how low-budget things were for us. At the end of the year, they sent me to San Antonio to tell him they'd like to bring him up for the rest of the year. He said, "Jimmy, I'd rather not. My arm is not sound right now. If I go up there and do bad, I may not get a chance in the spring." He was right about the arm. He did have the start of a problem that ultimately killed his career, but he did get his chance in spring training. He was with the club on the way to Detroit to open our first season in Baltimore when the

Orioles picked up Vern Bickford from the Braves and cut Vachel (and my $1,000).

I heard later that when we signed him, the Red Sox were ready to give him a bonus of about $5,000. We didn't give him anything. His dad turned the Boston money down and said, "That boy's got to start at the bottom, and he'll have a better chance with the Browns." We started him at the bottom all right—Wausau, Wisconsin, Class D.

Vachel always laughed about that signing. He told a friend of mine, "Jim wooed my dad. He had him all locked up. He got my dad, he didn't get me." Another thing he said that got back to me was: "Every time I talk to people about baseball, we talk about Jimmy. He started out here at this little Alma radio station and he was good enough and ambitious enough and smart enough to scout for World Series teams. I'd love to go to a ballgame with him sometime." I'd have loved that, too, but we waited too long. Vachel was back in Edmore, a successful businessman and community leader, when a rare nerve disease took his life in December 1991. He left behind a lovely family and an old baseball scout honored to have run across him, signed him and known him.

Not long after I signed Vachel, I was hired by a radio station in Riverside, California, where I did college football games and broke into baseball with the Riverside team in the Class C Sunset League, which also had clubs in places like Tijuana and Mexicali. I broadcast all the Riverside home games and recreated the road games. I enjoyed the broadcasting, but for the second time in a brief career I found that was the easy part of the job. The hard part was management. At Alma, the station was owned by a religious fanatic who wouldn't carry the Tigers games because of the beer advertisements. At Riverside, the station owner was almost broke. The broadcasting stars in my eyes burned out fast.

Still, Riverside was a good move for me because two great things happened. The traffic manager for the Riverside station was a lovely young lady who became my wife, Betty. And in the fall of 1951, the Browns took me on as a full-time scout.

Abandoning broadcasting to go into baseball took some guts, because by then we had started a family. I just always felt comfortable about myself when it came to baseball. I loved the game and tried to study it.

And it sure wasn't much of a gamble for the Browns. It wasn't likely that I was going to hurt them.

The last line on the dedication plaque at Memorial Stadium in Baltimore, put up in 1954, the year the Browns moved to Baltimore, says:

TIME WILL NOT DIM THE GLORY OF THEIR DEEDS.

Believe me, it refers to our military troops of the world wars, not to the St. Louis Browns. Nobody does a better job of handling publicity for a major league club than Bob Brown of the Orioles. In his press guide, Bob says the Browns ''were probably the most consistently bad club in major league history.'' How bad? One pennant and forty second-division finishes in a fifty-two year history; all told, more than 1,000 games below .500—a 67-87 *average* per season.

To this day, it's hard for me to believe how we conducted major league business in the St. Louis Browns organization. If we had operated on a shoestring, it would have been an improvement. We couldn't afford shoes.

It was awfully difficult to compete in those days, because really we didn't. It was made very clear to me, right from the beginning, that the Browns just did not have money. ''You're going to have to get your ballplayers out of tryout camps. We have no bonus money to give. None.''

I was assigned to Texas and Oklahoma, good baseball states. Ada, Oklahoma, was one of our Class D clubs, and naturally a team at that bottom-of-the-line level was always losing players—through promotion, or discouraged kids just going home, or having to tell a young man he'd better find another line of work because he just wasn't good enough for even there. With all that attrition, the team had to be maintained, and I was told I had to supply the replacement players. The expense of signing a ballplayer in, say, New England and flying him to Ada was prohibitive to the Browns. I had to find players nearby, from tryout camps. (Playing at Ada was another thing. The field had *no* grass, because it was a rodeo ground. They had the only bonafide bullpen I ever saw. The relief pitchers warmed up in the pen where the bulls were kept before being turned loose— and those bulls left behind what you expect them to leave behind. Probably no bullpen in the history of the game ever made relievers more conscious of their footwork.)

So, sometimes at Ada, sometimes not, in 96- or 98-degree heat and dust that made you choke, I ran one-man tryout camps. I would register all the kids, then judge them on the two things that can't be taught: speed and strength of arm. You could eliminate damned near all of them right there. Then, with the rest, I would draw up teams and pitch each pitcher one or two innings—or, maybe an extra inning or so for a pitcher who looked promising. After all, we weren't limited to playing nine innings; we could go on and on and on.

That meant I might have to judge hitters on just a few swings, but that was enough to tell if a pretty good stroke was there. I could see a guy strike out four times and still like his swing. What you're seeing is what you think it takes to play in the big leagues successfully. You're never real sure, obviously. There's always a percentage of mistakes. You might see what a player has outwardly, and you're enthused about what he's showing you—the speed is there, the arm is there, he takes a good cut. You say to yourself, "Hey, this guy really looks like something." But you're not sure what's inside. You don't know if he has the heart, or the stomach—and I think they both wind up being pretty much the same thing.

I can remember Wisconsin had an outfielder by the name of John DeMerit. Whenever anyone uses that tag "can't-miss," I think of John DeMerit and shake my head. He looked good in everything he did and the way he did it—the good cut, the poise, the speed, and he'd catch the ball, and he could throw it. He just looked like "money in the bank." But in five very brief big league trials, he hit .174 and washed out. A few years later in the same college league, Kirk Gibson came along at Michigan State—not blessed with as many tools as DeMerit had, not the best thrower and not a tremendous outfielder by any means. But he's turned out to be nineteen times better than DeMerit, and he has a spot in the game's history. His ninth-inning first-game home run off Dennis Eckersley gave the 1988 World Series such a violent turnaround that one of the best of today's managers, Tony LaRussa, couldn't get things back in place and wound up losing the Series to a team that wasn't as good as his A's. People say one swing did it, but my scouting instincts tell me what really did it was that Mr. Gibson had the heart and the stomach that you'd die to find in a good prospect, but you can't tell if it's there till the guy gets out and starts playing.

There are things you look for when evaluating a kid: No. 1, does he have those things I can't teach him—how does he run, throw, hit the ball? Does he have an instinct for the game?

I always liked to size him up a little beyond what I could see by sitting down and talking to him to find out if he's genuinely interested in professional baseball, and a lot of little things in personal makeup that can be helpful—but not the final answer. You get the final answer when they start throwing the baseball 90 miles an hour. Then he's on his own, and until then, you can't be 100 percent sure.

Oh, you make mistakes, and I certainly made my share. Anyone in scouting who says he never made one is playing games with the truth. But obviously you want to keep your mistakes down to a minimum, because if you make too many, it's "See you later."

Then there are times, very rare but very special, when you just *know*.

That was the romance of it. Don't let me kid you about the working conditions. Yeah, it was uncomfortable, even miserable. But on those days in that heat and dirt I knew exactly how those California and Alaska gold-panners felt, because there was always the chance of a strike.

I used to tell the scouts who worked under me, "Trust what your experience and your heart tell you, because if you see a player that you *really* like, you'll not only see him with your eyes but feel it in your heart."

And you feel it a little bit lower when you realize you let one of those get away.

I remember watching the Southern League All-Star Game at Nashville, and there was a pitcher out there throwing a ball that looked like a little pea. We didn't use speed guns in those days, but he had to be throwing in the nineties. I watched him for a little longer and I began to get a sick feeling because I knew who he was. A few years earlier, I had a tryout camp in San Antonio, and this kid was there. Sure, there were a lot of ballplayers to look at, about 175, but I missed him. The player was Gary Bell, who went on to a darned good career with the Indians and Red Sox. He just threw the hell out of the ball that night at Nashville, and I knew right then I should have been sharper back there on that field in San Antonio. I thought, "Oh, God, no. How could he have gotten this much faster? I can't believe it." Our farm director, Jim McLaughlin, had a theory that a pitcher threw as hard at eighteen as he was ever going to throw. I liked Jimmy McLaughlin, but the Gary Bells convinced me he was dead wrong about that.

And if Gary Bell way back then wasn't a convincer, how about Nolan Ryan, the pitching wonder of the 1990s?

Ryan came out of Alvin, Texas, in 1965, and we were never on him. I later asked our scout from there, Dee Phillips, what had happened. Dee said he knew about him and had looked at him. But he not only didn't throw like the Ryan of the 1960s, 1970s, 1980s and 1990s, he was also skinny. I'll never have a better refutation to cite in arguing against the McLaughlin theory than Ryan. From what I saw in his seventh no-hitter, at age forty-four, I'm not sure Ryan's not *still* getting faster.

As for Gary Bell, whether I could have signed him if I had spotted the talent at that tryout camp, I can't be sure, but it wasn't like the Brownie days. Then, we had no money to give out, and it wasn't an act. There were times when the Browns, to meet their own payroll, had to draw from the San Antonio account. The secretaries in the St. Louis office told me bills would come in with the word ''please'' on them. Any billpayer knows that means it is long overdue.

We were told to sign our players for $150 a month, which in the early 1950s wasn't a bad salary for a young professional ballplayer. I tried to use our situation as a plus. I'd tell kids they could get to the majors faster with the Browns than any other club—we didn't even have a Triple-A team to go through. For the really good ones, I'd promise them if they'd sign with us, play one summer and do well, we'd take them to big league camp the next year. If they were impressive there, they could be in the big leagues their third or fourth year in baseball. I told that to Ralph Terry, and he was enthused about it. The next time I saw him, he was gracious but said, "Mr. Russo, I'm going to have to sign with somebody else." The Yankees had offered him the spring training chance, *and* a big bonus.

Maybe it's hard to believe, but those were happy times. Truly professional owners made it that way—Bill and Charlie DeWitt when I first joined the club, then Bill Veeck in my last three years.

The DeWitts were just great baseball men and—if money isn't the big thing you're in the game for, and it surely wasn't for many scouts—great people to be around, to work for and with.

And Bill Veeck. God love him. It was a great day for all of baseball when they finally found a spot in Cooperstown for a man who bridged the gap between fan and front office better than anyone I met in thirty-five years in professional baseball.

I got to know him better when he owned the White Sox the second time, in the 1970s. What a fine, fine person. He would hold court at a table in the Bards' Room (the press/hospitality room) in Comiskey Park, before and after games but mostly after—especially night games. He was so exciting to listen to that one hour led to another which led to another which led to another. By the time you looked at your watch, you'd been there four hours. And if you were drinking beer with him, you were in trouble.

He loved beer. He'd sit there and sip. You'd swear to God he was drinking water. People always wondered if it was going into that wooden leg. How the hell could you sit there sipping beer in the afternoon, the latter stages of the afternoon, during the game, and then maybe for four hours after the game and still be coherent? He didn't gulp it down, he sipped it, but nevertheless he'd have that fresh glass pretty often. You start figuring it up and that's a lot of beer.

He ran his ballclubs like no one else, ever. Right to the end, the average fan could call the main White Sox switchboard number, ask for Bill Veeck and get him, directly. He always had time for baseball fans. It wasn't easy for him to get around, after losing a leg to cancer, but every now and then he'd pop up sitting in the centerfield bleachers, shirt off, soaking up sun and suds— rooting and chatting and second-guessing with his people, the fans.

He was tireless. Those nights that he drank and talked the rest of us into exhaustion after games, he might have begun the day by talking to one, two or three different groups—and he might have one, two or three more lined up to hear him the next morning. And he didn't just talk. He had the most beautiful way of phrasing things of anyone in the game. He was a fine, fine person, and Mary Frances, his wife, was just lovely. Bill knew there were owners that didn't like him, and he knew why. But he somehow always gave me the impression that he held no animosity toward them. Maybe there was some, deep down. But maybe there wasn't. The ones dumb enough to resent having Bill Veeck in baseball he might have figured were dumb enough for him to beat, whether he had money or not.

It's funny that I always picture Bill sipping a beer, because beer was his final downfall in St. Louis. A stubborn man, as well as a beautifully inventive soul, he might have gone ahead and battled the Cardinals for support in St. Louis, a great baseball city, forever. But when the Cards were sold to Gussie Busch, Bill knew it was over. There was no way we could fight a brewery. In 1953, our last year there, things were really tough. We drew less than 300,000, which is a good homestand for the Cardinals now. But even though the bills were coming in with "Please" on them, we in the organization always got paid on time. Never, never, never late. And he was the perfect guy to work for in another respect. If you did your job, he never bothered you.

Bill spent that bleak 1953 season trying to make the Baltimore move himself. But the fellow owners he had delighted in gigging over the years had him in a perfect position. He couldn't move without their permission, and they put the squeeze on him. Finally, on Sept. 29, 1953, they had their way. He sold control of the club to Baltimore interests, and the first American League franchise shift in fifty-two years sailed through quickly and smoothly.

Veeck, of course, got back into baseball—first with the White Sox, when they won their first pennant in forty years in 1959, then after getting forced out by illness, back with the White Sox again in the 1970s.

I thought one more time of Bill in the summer of 1989 when the White Sox traded Harold Baines to Texas. I believe that removed the last on-field link between Veeck and the White Sox, and it was a classic Bill Veeck link. In his forced absence from the game in the 1970s, Veeck convalesced at his home on Maryland's Eastern Shore and couldn't stay away from ballparks. He used to tell those Bards' Room crowds how he was at a Little League game one time and saw a twelve-year-old boy hit the ball 400 feet, clear over one Little League diamond and almost out of another one that was adjacent to it. He made a note of that boy's name, and in 1977, when everyone was saying the two hot picks were Bill Gullickson, a young high school pitcher from the Chicago suburbs, and Paul Molitor, a shortstop with the University of Minnesota, Veeck had first pick for the White Sox and took Harold Baines of St. Michaels (Md.) High School.

Everybody said he was pinching pennies at his team's expense, dodging the big money that Gullickson (the No. 2 pick, by Montreal) and Molitor (No. 3, by Milwaukee) would command. But Veeck pulled off something that made all of us old Browns proud, because he did save money by taking Baines— and, as good as Gullickson and Molitor turned out to be, Baines, though maybe slightly below Molitor in pure ability, has been the best of the three. When Baines left in that 1989 trade, it was

one of the smartest moves the White Sox could have made because it brought in youth, speed, defense and pitching, critical
elements in building a team at Comiskey Park—the old one or
the new one.

And still, down deep I have the feeling that if Bill Veeck had
been running the White Sox, it wouldn't have happened. Veeck
was too much of a romanticist to cut his ties with Harold Baines.
Ever.

3

An Occasional Curve

You never know what you'll have to fight when you go out to sign a player.

In 1964, the last year before the free-agent draft, our Texas scout, Dee Phillips, told me there was a pretty good shortstop at Palestine that he'd like me to cross-check, because if we wanted him, we were going to have to work quick. The kid was a good quarterback, too, and Darrell Royal wanted him at Texas.

Dee, who is with the Tigers now, is one of the best scouts in baseball, so when he wanted me to get on something, I got on it.

I watched the boy play a baseball game, and it was obvious he had pretty good ability and good size—about 6-feet, 185 pounds, as I remember.

We made an appointment and went to his home. The boy wasn't there—he was in school or somewhere—so our meeting was with his mother. Obviously it's best to have the player there, but in this case it didn't make any difference because his mother had plenty to say.

I gave her our thinking and told her things about the Baltimore organization. And I told her he would have to make a decision, because if he stayed with football, he risked being injured to the point where his baseball career would be finished.

I said to her, "You indicate to me he wants to play baseball?"

"Oh, yes, Mr. Russo, he certainly does. And we think he's the best baseball player in this state."

Most mothers do, and I've never argued *that* point with one yet.

I said, "Suppose he's hurt. Injuries happen all the time in football—it could be a knee, an ankle, a shoulder."

She said, "Mr. Russo, Coach Royal was in our home, sitting in the same chair that you're sitting in, and he told us that Texas was going to have such an outstanding line that nobody would ever lay a hand on Billy."

I just looked at her. I couldn't believe I'd heard her right. I said, "Would you repeat that?" She said, "That's the truth, Mr. Russo. We trust Mr. Royal and that's exactly what he told us."

She wasn't joking.

I'd heard there were places in Texas where they thought Darrell could part the sea, and obviously we were sitting in one.

Then she said, "Not only that, Mr. Russo, we think that he is so good that he won't ever have to see the minor leagues. When he leaves Texas he will go right to the big leagues."

I thought, "Russo, forget it. There's no way you're going to win this one."

When we left, I told Dee, "Now you see what we're up against, when a college coach can come in here and leave them completely captivated."

The boy went to Texas, and the next thing I heard was that Royal's great line had failed the kid. He tore up a knee, and we tore up our scouting report—one more career down the drain.

Except...

The kid's name was Bill Bradley. No, he's not the U.S. senator, but when he had to give up quarterback and shortstop, this Bill Bradley switched to the defensive secondary, and darned if he didn't stick in the NFL for nine years—a couple of them all-pro. And to this day in Texas, he's still known as Super Bill.

The story is still told in Texas of the time the great University of Texas sports publicity director Jones Ramsey was out of town and a tornado hit Austin. His Texas friends swear that Jones called his wife and the worried conversation from his end went:

"Honey, I heard about the storm. How's Super Bill?"

"Good...good..."

"And, oh, by the way...how are you and the kids?"

That kid must have been Super.

I went to Memphis in June of 1959 with $60,000 to offer to a good-looking young catcher just out of high school. You've heard of him: Tim McCarver, who had a good major league career but has hit it bigger by far as a network TV analyst.

Tim signed with the Birds, but not the Baltimore kind. I don't know what he got to sign with the St. Louis Cardinals, but he never found out what I had to offer, either. We had the shortest negotiating session in history.

Even then, at eighteen, Tim was a poised, articulate, organized young man. He knew he was marketable, and he didn't sit on his porch waiting for baseball folks to drop by. He set up headquarters for two days in a Memphis hotel.

When my appointment time came, I walked in the room and saw not just Tim but also Will Carruthers, a Memphis sportswriter whom I knew—very well.

I said, "Tim, I'm prepared to make you a legitimate offer on behalf of the Baltimore Orioles, but I won't make it until Mr. Carruthers leaves the room."

Tim looked genuinely astonished, but not at all flustered. Very coolly, he said, "Mr. Carruthers is a friend of the family, and he is advising me. I see no harm in him being here."

"If he stays," I responded, "I will leave, and I won't present our offer."

"Mr. Russo," Tim said, "I think very highly of you and your organization, but Mr. Carruthers stays."

And Mr. Russo didn't.

Why?

Will Carruthers was a good sportswriter and a good guy,

but he wasn't just working for his newspaper. He also was helping the Cardinals. I knew whatever offer I made would be passed along to the Cardinals, who would know just exactly what they had to do to top not only us but any other bidders.

It wasn't general knowledge that Carruthers was helping the Cardinals, but I knew—because gathering inside information was part of my job. When Jim McLaughlin was running our scouting, he was constantly trying to get across to all of us that we could never have too much information on a prospective player. To make his point at one of our winter organization meetings, he brought in FBI agents to teach us some intelligence-gathering tricks—get to know the girl friend, the player's buddies, the high school coach. Figuring out that Carruthers was a Cardinal plant in the McCarver dealing was nickel-and-dime stuff compared to some of the things those FBI guys talked about.

The postscript to all of that is that McCarver did, indeed, sign with the Cardinals—for a reported $75,000.

I got to know Tim well over the years, well enough that we rehashed that hotel room scene and both laughed about it. He agreed that if he had been in my position, he'd have taken a walk, too. And I agreed that he and Carruthers both must have known what they were doing. In those days, $75,000 was a lot of money for a guy who could run, hit and catch, with slightly below average arm strength but the savvy to disguise it with an exceptionally quick release. He turned out to be worth it—and I'll bet he's talking a lot bigger numbers now as CBS's golden boy.

Sometimes you don't have to look very far at all to find an absolute jewel.

During my Orioles years, Cal Ripken was a coach with us, and every now and then his son—about fourteen, already tall and rangy—would take batting practice. Even then you could see that Cal, Jr., had a chance to be pretty good. But lots of kids have a chance. Not many kids are like Cal Ripken, Jr.

Of all the guys in the major leagues right now, he may be my favorite player. He just keeps getting better, and smarter, and he started out at a pretty high level in both categories.

It's looking more and more like he could get one of those records that seemed absolutely unassailable: Lou Gehrig's 2,130 consecutive games played. I never met Gehrig, but the kind of man I've always heard he was fits pretty closely with the Cal Ripken I know: great competitor, always gives everything he has, and still is unfailingly polite and a gentleman in every way imaginable—and some that go beyond that. When baseball set up as a memorial to the late commissioner the Bart Giamatti Caring Award, the first recipient (in December 1989) was Cal Ripken, Jr. That year, he and his wife, Kelly, contributed $250,000 when the city of Baltimore established an adult literacy program and agreed to match any other donations. Even at today's salaries, that's a huge gift, and Cal gives an even more precious asset, his time, to hospitals in the area. Several years ago, he and Eddie Murray each started giving away twenty-five tickets for every home game, and Cal has kept that up. He's a very special man.

I have to confess if I'd had my way, Cal would be building his legends as a third baseman. I never doubted his ability to play shortstop. How could you?

But I looked at young Cal (6-4, 215) and I remembered another Oriole shortstop: Ron Hansen (6-3, 190). Ronnie had a good career, but it was complicated and shortened by back problems that ultimately led to a triple spinal fusion operation. I always felt his problem was linked to all the quick, lateral moves, the jolting stops, the twists and the throws from awkward positions that a shortstop has to make. To me, it's a position that fits an Aparicio (5-9, 160) a lot better than it does a Hansen or Ripken.

So, I suggested we make Cal a third baseman.

The suggestion never got very far. Earl Weaver said, ''Are you kidding me? He's a shortstop, he's going to stay at shortstop, and he'll play it all the way to Cooperstown.''

I think he's right about that. But they do allow third basemen in there, too.

4

Learning to Cope

When the Browns were sold to Bill Veeck, we were able to increase the scouting staff, so I was moved around: from southern California, where my wife and I got married, to Texas and then in 1955 to Ohio, because the health of one of my early benefactors, P.L. McCormick, was deteriorating. I lived in Bellefontaine, just north of Springfield, for three years, and then in 1958 they put me in charge of scouting in twenty-six midwest and western states. With my promotion came a move to St. Louis, where I've lived ever since.

In Texas and Oklahoma, I learned some of the ropes and had a lot of help. One of the first to give me a hand when it mattered was Wog Rice, a longtime Boston scout. Wog lived in Norman, Oklahoma, and he was a good friend of the biggest man in that whole area then, Oklahoma football coach Bud Wilkinson. Every spring in Norman, they had a gigantic high school baseball tournament—about sixty teams, playing on nine fields, all over the Norman area. The first year I went in there, I was overwhelmed, and Wog Rice saw that immediately. He introduced himself and said, ''You're kinda confused, aren't you?'' I said I sure was, and he sat down, pulled out the schedule and the rosters, and said, "Now, you make sure you see this guy, and this guy...there's a pitcher named Lindy McDaniel, make sure you see him...and this guy, and this guy." You can't believe how big a help that was. It automatically eliminated all the schools that I might have been looking at unnecessarily, hoping I might find something that looked halfway decent. I never forgot that. I tried to remember it when I saw other young scouts looking a little dazed. And from that day on, Wog Rice had himself a friend.

I also met Tom Greenwade, the Yankee scout who signed Mickey Mantle, and Hugh Alexander, who was with the Dodgers then. Greenwade told me one time, in my Brownie days, "You deserve a lot of credit. You have to work three times harder than the rest of us because you have to find that needle in a haystack out there." I grabbed at a couple of needles. I signed a pitcher named Johnny Wartelle, and I think he may still hold the strikeout record in the Big State League—19, for Paris one night. I also signed a left-hander named Rhodes—every Rhodes is nicknamed Dusty, and that's the best I can do for a first name. All I remember is he set some sort of control record in the Sooner State League for Ada. But Wartelle hurt his arm and Rhodes' fastball wasn't good enough, so neither made the big leagues.

By the time I got to Ohio, our club had some money and nobody felt sorry for the new kid breaking in. Bob "Buck" Rodgers, who much later was to become one of baseball's better managers, came along as a top prospect in Delaware, Ohio, not far from where I lived. I liked him; everybody did—a strong, good-looking catcher. Wayne Blackburn, the Tigers' scout, took him into Detroit to work him out, but when they came back Rodgers said he was going to go to college and not sign. I talked to him; same thing. "I'm going to school." It was believable. Rules at the time said any player signed for a bonus above $4,000 had to go right onto the 25-man major league roster. It was a rule designed to hold down the spending, because putting even one kid on the big club's roster who couldn't play put the team at a disadvantage. The only problem with the rule was it made liars out of a lot of people. The *listed* bonus was always $4,000, but the money that changed hands—in a wide, imaginative variety of ways—was as high as ever, considerably above $4,000.

However, several weeks after Bob Rodgers said he was going to college, I had a bad kidney infection that put me flat on my back. That's where I was when I heard on the radio that the Tigers had signed him. Wayne Blackburn was a good friend of mine, so I called him: "You no-good son of a bitch, you're telling everybody he isn't going to sign, and while I'm flat on my back, you sign him—and I know God-damned well you probably gave him a bunch of money under the table." He said, "Oh, no, not more than the limit." By then, it was really just a lot of fun—but it did involve a good ballplayer. The funny thing is the Tigers didn't get him, either. He was at Triple-A when they lost him in the expansion draft to the Angels. So they had to hurry up and break in another young kid who wasn't too bad: Bill Freehan.

My job introduced me to some great people. The first time I met Fred Taylor, the Hall of Fame basketball coach at Ohio State, he was raking the infield after a rain to help his old baseball coach there, Marty Karow, get a game in. Freddie had a chance to make it as a player himself, but he came along as a Senators first baseman behind Mickey Vernon. Bad timing, except for basketball, which got a hell of a coach out of that situation. I was in Columbus to see another pretty good basketball player, Paul Ebert, who I thought was just an outstanding pitching prospect. I followed Paul all the way to Mexico City for the Pan American Games. I was crazy about him—tall, lean, the Jim Palmer type, good arm, a hell of a curve ball. People said, "Don't expect to see a good curve ball down there because the air is so thin." Hell, his curve was as good as I had seen it in Ohio. I really got excited then. I even asked former Ohio governor Jim Rhodes to help me, because I knew he was a big sports fan and he knew Ebert.

Unfortunately for us, Paul was even better on academic curves. He passed up our offer to go to medical school—I had even offered to pay for that. Last I heard he was director of the

American College of Surgeons, so I guess he didn't make a mistake. Had a hell of a curve ball, though.

When I got my promotion in 1958 and moved to St. Louis, I had fourteen scouts under me working pretty much the western two-thirds of the country.

I had good people working with me, and I had something I wanted to try out on them. I had the feeling by then that we were on the verge of something pretty good, and a lot of my guys were like me, left over from the days when we were forced to take what we could get. I wanted them to raise their sights, but I knew saying that wouldn't get the job done.

We had a fall meeting one year, and I said, "Don't ever write me or call me and say 'Jim, I've got a hell of a player here that I think can play in the big leagues.' A lot of guys can play in the big leagues. I want you to tell me if we can beat the Yankees with your ballplayer."

They knew exactly what I meant, but I spelled it out: "There are two types of big-league ballplayers, first division and second division. If you have too many second-division players, that's exactly where you finish. We want FIRST-division players. Your mistakes will become second-division players."

I think it had the impact I wanted. The Yankees were riding high then, first or second every year, and we hadn't been anyplace yet. But check the history. We overtook them; for a thirty year period, we had the best record in the major leagues. And maybe you didn't notice it but I'll guarantee you I did and all the guys working with me did: when we won the World Series in 1966, we had two great players we had picked up in trades, Frank Robinson and Luis Aparicio, but most of that club came right out of our farm system—and the key men in the deals that got us Robinson and Aparicio came from the system. We beat the Yankees, with our ballplayers.

I was on the go all the time then, coming in to take a look at kids our area scouts had seen and recommended. I would spend ten days or more in southern California alone to look at the guys our scouts liked out there. That seems like a lot of time, but they're all over the place out there. Where at one time I had four midwestern states, in the Los Angeles area alone, we had two full-time scouts, and they had associate scouts under them.

One of the first jobs I remember in my supervisory assignment was checking out Ron Fairly at Southern Cal. Our scouts loved him, and it happened that USC was going to play against our Triple-A team, Vancouver, which was training at Riverside, California. I did some checking and found out that George Bamberger was going to start the game for Vancouver. George had had just a little taste of the majors (he came up with Bobby Thomson's Giants team in 1951) but he was a tough, old Triple-A pitcher, absorbing all the things that later made him one of the greatest pitching coaches in the game. I knew he had outstanding control, and I asked him to do me a favor: "Ron Fairly is going to get a ton of money from someone. I'd like to learn as much as I can about him, so I'd appreciate it if you'd bust one under his chin, knock him down." George didn't even smile. He said, "Yeah, I can do that."

First time up, here came the ball at Fairly's chin and down he went. Second pitch, he lined a shot off the right-field wall. That told me everything I needed to know about Ron Fairly, and he turned out to be just as good a hitter as I thought he'd be— but for the Dodgers, who won that battle, not us.

We won our share, sometimes head-to-head with the Dodgers.

That's what it worked down to for Dave McNally, when he came along in Billings, Montana. Billings had no high school baseball because of the cold spring weather but the summer American Legion program was one of the best anywhere. The coach was a good baseball man, Ed Bayne, who the last I heard was in his seventies and, thirty years after McNally, still coaching the team. He ran a first-class program. This was 1960, and the Billings Legion team then traveled in an air-conditioned luxury bus similar to what rock groups and country/western stars travel in now.

McNally was a hot name. He had been in the Legion World Series two years earlier. This was his last year of high school, and every club in baseball knew about him. It was obvious he was going to sign, and the figure was going to be big—maybe $100,000.

Jim Wilson, who pitched for the Orioles and for several other big league clubs, was the Orioles' California scout, in his first year of scouting but already a good one. He later was director of the Major League Scouting Bureau. He liked McNally a lot. So did two other scouts we had look at him: Byron Humphrey, who was one of the best scouts I had under me, and Burleigh Grimes, who was known in baseball as the last legal spitball pitcher but was damned good as a scout, too. Jim McLaughlin told me to join the other three guys at Hastings, Nebraska, to see McNally in the American Legion World Series and decide whether he was worth pursuing at the price it was going to take.

Before I got there, he pitched twice in the Series; he struck out 19 in the first game and 17 in the second, and gave up 6 hits in the two games together. I got there for the championship game: McNally and Billings against New Orleans with Rusty Staub (it was a good Series for scouts; Pittsfield, Massachusetts, was in it with a sixteen-year-old shortstop named Mark Belanger). McNally looked tired to me—not as fast as I had been led to expect. But, damn, it was his third game in a week; he surely was tired. And he was snapping off one of the best curve balls I had ever seen on a seventeen-year-old. An old baseball truism ran through my mind: lefties don't have to throw as hard as right-handed pitchers. And, occasionally he would pop a live fastball, so I felt that he had shown me enough pitches, plus great poise and polish, that we wanted to go after him hard. He lost, 3-2, to finish his season 18-1. Wilson and I headed for Billings with a Monday night appointment to meet the McNallys.

Dave's dad had been killed in the South Pacific in World War II, when Dave was two years old. When Wilson and I arrived at the family home, the McNallys were there and so was the man who was to act as adviser and agent: Cale Crowley, considered the top criminal lawyer in the state. I told Wilson, ''This will not be easy.''

Crowley and Dave's dad had been very close. Crowley told us the only time in his life that he ever cried was when he learned Dave's dad had been killed.

I made my pitch straight at Dave, selling the Orioles and our need for pitching. Dave sat across the room and never said a word or asked a question, yet I had no doubt he was absorbing everything I said. Crowley and all, I felt Dave would make the final choice.

The Dodgers had preceded me and their opening offer was $75,000. That thinned out the table. A lot of clubs were in town, eager to make a presentation, before the Dodger offer got around. Several of them left—among them the Yankees, of all people. When CBS took over ownership of the club, the word got around that some genius of broadcasting had put a new operating rule into effect: from that day forward, the Yankees would give no *pitcher* a bonus over $50,000, because a pitcher could come up with a bad arm and the money would be wasted.

That was the first time I honestly felt sure we could overtake them.

No club can have a rule that dumb and stay where the Yankees had been. But it evidently was true; with the bidding at $75,000, the Yankees were one of the clubs that cut and ran.

McLaughlin and I had discussed money and we felt $80,000 was a fair figure. After what he saw in Hastings, Grimes was ready to go higher: "Whatever it takes." I said, "Burleigh, we *have* to stop somewhere." McLaughlin's last words to me from Baltimore were: "Don't lose him."

I gave the McNallys our offer: $80,000 for a bonus, and a salary that was negotiable. Crowley said they would consider the offer and get back to us. Wednesday, he called and said we were in the ballpark but they still had clubs to talk with. The next day, Crowley and an accountant came to our hotel and told us the Dodgers had offered $90,000. I spent another hour selling the Orioles and told Crowley that we weren't going to get in a bidding war, and taxes would take most of the $10,000 difference, anyway. Crowley said Dave would make his decision the next day.

Meanwhile, McLaughlin was calling once or twice daily telling me not to lose McNally. "If it takes more money, we have it." I told him, too, that I didn't want to get in a bidding contest.

(Now, let's stop right here and get something straight. I wasn't *that* protective of Orioles money. I just felt very strongly that whatever bid we made, the Dodgers would top, so we weren't going to win if things went that way. We had to fight this one out on different grounds, and I felt if I could do that, I had the edge. After all, I was an old Brown.)

Friday came, and I was sick. *Really* sick—diarrhea, nausea, vomiting, the whole thing. I fought my way to a pharmacy to try to get something that would help. The pharmacist looked at me and said, "Are you a baseball scout?" The question kind of shocked me, but the way I was feeling I didn't challenge him on it, I just said, "Yes."

He broke out laughing. "I thought so," he said. "Two other scouts have been in already this morning complaining about the same thing. The only thing wrong with you guys is you're feeling the pressure." He got me some Kaopectate and as he handed it to me, he just shook his head. "Dam-nation. I knew Dave was a hell of a pitcher, but I didn't know he was *that* good."

Crowley and his accountant came to our hotel on Friday afternoon. I knew this would be our last shot, and after the morning I had gone through, I was *glad* it was. But, by the time we had our meeting, the pharmacist's Kaopectate had done its job, and I was beyond worrying about having to interrupt negotiations to make an indelicate but quick exit.

Crowley asked us to increase the bonus, and I told him I felt our offer was sufficient and went over my reasons again—although I think I forgot to mention the one about not wanting to get into a bidding war with the Dodgers. I thought it was audacious to make the taxes-will-eat-up-the-difference argument with an accountant present, but maybe the thing did fall right into a tax breakpoint because darned if the guy didn't let me get away with it—not actually agreeing, but not saying as I halfway expected him to say, "Bullshit. You pay the money and we'll worry about taxes." I'm not sure what I would have done if he had, because again that very morning, McLaughlin had called and said those magic words: "Don't you lose McNally." Don't *you* lose McNally. My good buddy Jim was making this thing uncomfortably personal.

Crowley listened, said he would call and give us Dave's decision, and I knew he was ready to leave. It flashed through my mind: "This is it. Give it your best shot."

I walked across the room to directly in front of Crowley, who still was seated, and looked straight into his eyes. "You told us the only time in your life that you ever cried was when you learned Dave's father had died," I said. "I'll tell you how strongly I believe in what we've told you. If you let Dave go with any club other than the Orioles, his dad will turn over in his grave."

He gave me a strange sort of look, got up and left, saying he would get back with us.

My performance did not win an Oscar from Jim Wilson. "Well," he said, "we've lost him. How in the hell could you *say* something like that?"

Down deep, I knew there was a chance he could be right— that I could have totally turned Crowley off. But I told Wilson what I had told myself: "This man is a trial lawyer. He has to appeal to a jury when he is trying to save a client from the gallows or the electric chair or the rope on a tree branch or whatever the hell Montana uses for ultimate justice now. I tried to speak his language." I still felt the final decision would be Dave's, but I knew he and Cale had gone too far down the road together for Dave not to listen to Crowley's last bit of advice.

In thirty minutes, Cale Crowley knocked on the door. He said, "He's yours. He wants to go with the Orioles."

"But couldn't you search your heart for $5,000 more."

By then, *especially* then, I loved the kid. But damned if I didn't say no. Old Brownies never die.

I did make sure Dave received a salary that was a whole lot heftier than it might have been. He got his money, *after* the bidding.

The McNallys held a party that night at their home. What a beautiful family, just truly delightful. During the evening, I said to Crowley, "By the way, if I'm ever up for murder, I want you to defend me."

He just laughed and said, "We'd both hang."

The McNally chase had an interesting postscript. At the winter meetings the year after that, Burt Wells, who was scouting supervisor for the Dodgers, accused me of telling the McNallys, "You don't want to go with the Dodgers. In Dodgertown at Vero Beach, they sleep the blacks and the whites together." He said he knew for a fact that they had been told that, and "You must have said it, because you got the ballplayer."

My hair stood straight up then. I was mad. I told him, "Listen, God dammit, the Orioles don't have to stoop to tactics like that, and I personally wouldn't do it. If someone said it, it sure as hell wasn't me or anyone with the Orioles."

He was still upset, and Hugh Alexander, a great scout now with the Cubs but working with the Dodgers at the time, said, "Just a minute, Burt. If Jimmy says he didn't say it, then, dammit, he didn't say it. I've known Jimmy a long time and he doesn't do stuff like that."

A couple of years later, when McNally was pitching for us in the big leagues, I had a chance to sit down with him when no one else was present and I brought this up. I said, "Dave, in the negotiations, when you were getting ready to sign—I've been accused of saying you shouldn't go with the Dodgers because they let the blacks sleep with the whites in Vero Beach. You know I never said anything like that." He said, "It was said, but it sure as hell wasn't by you." I never asked him who, but the fact that things worked out the way they did told me the McNallys were the kind of people I thought they were all along. Whoever even brought up that kind of racist nonsense apparently was eliminated early. After all, it *was* fourteen years after Jackie Robinson.

• 5

Richards, Money, and The Babe

The St. Louis Browns became the Baltimore Orioles in 1954, but the real Oriole story began a year later. That's when Paul Rapier Richards arrived, promised that he would be given an open checkbook to work with. It was an all new way of living for our franchise. I've talked about the challenge, the romance, of squeezing every nickel with the Browns. At the same time, I always felt we had the talent in our organization to be able to compete, if we'd had just a little bit more money. All of a sudden, with Paul Richards, we had more than a little bit. We had it to throw around, and did. And we competed. Sometimes with each other.

Paul was the biggest spender of all. He was the manager of the ballclub, and the general manager, and sometimes he acted as the head of his own Orioles farm system, although we already had one in place that was headed by Jim McLaughlin. It didn't take long before we had two factions at work rounding up players, the Richards faction and the McLaughlin faction. I was with McLaughlin, although it was a difficult situation in which to try to perform, because Richards had the authority to fire you. My allegiance was to McLaughlin, though, and I also happened to concur with most of his philosophy.

We wasted a lot of money in the early Richards years, a tremendous amount of money. Jim Keelty was the majority owner who took over as president in the front office upheaval that brought Richards in. Eventually, Keelty himself sold out, because he thought, "This man might break me."

Richards and his people were just throwing the money all over, promiscuously, and they didn't care a whole lot about following rules. Oklahoma State had a left-handed pitcher Paul liked. His name was Tom Borland, and Paul pitched him in an exhibition game under the name Moreland. That got out. We didn't get him.

We did get Bruce Swango, or he got us. Paul sent Dutch Dietrich—one of McLaughlin's scouts but a Richards man—in to see Swango, and the weather was bad so Dutch worked him out in a gymnasium. Dutch had to know better than to judge a pitcher on what he does in a gymnasium. If he's got even a mediocre fastball, the ball hitting that glove echoes off every wall in the place. Sound—that kind anyway, the pop into a catcher's glove that sounds as clean and sharp and loud as a rifle firing—has tricked more than one baseball man into snapping up a prospect. (It didn't always have to be in a gym. In my days with the Browns, the club sometimes would bring a kid from not too far away into St. Louis and work him out in the stadium. Les Moss, a catcher with the club then, used to play his own trick on the club. He'd get a kid with a pretty good fastball, and he'd tell him, "I'm going to get you a couple hundred dollars bonus." Les would get a brand new glove and make that ball sound like it was going 100 miles an hour. More than once, Bill DeWitt would be standing nearby, not paying a lot of attention, then hear that zing and say, "Did you hear that? We can't let this kid out of the ballpark without signing him." Les Moss may have been baseball's first agent.)

The Swango story became a classic because it wasn't long after we put him on a mound—after we had signed him to an $80,000 bonus—that we found out he had only one weakness.

He couldn't pitch. Two months after we gave him all that money, Paul released him, without ever pitching him in a professional game. The cover story Paul put out was that Swango was a nervous guy who could pitch on the sidelines but not in front of crowds. The truth was he couldn't get the ball over the plate even in batting practice. Paul never even blinked about wasting that money. (The funny thing with Swango was that he stayed at it and got another chance in the Yankee system—and three years after we let him go, he pitched a no-hitter for Fargo-Moorhead in the Northern League. Maybe they played the game in a gym.)

Then there was the time Paul's people signed Babe Ruth.

Paul heard about this high school kid in Dallas, and the more he heard the more he got excited. You can't believe how many guys he sent in there to look at him. One of them told Paul, "Honest to God, he looks like Babe Ruth up there." And that became his code name—The Babe. Richards just fell in love with him, and signed him—for big money, naturally. "Lord knows how good this kid is going to be," Paul would say. "It's unbelievable." His coaches, Jimmy Adair and Luman Harris, would get excited right along with him.

They brought the kid to spring training, right out of high school. He was all anybody was talking about—The Babe, how much he hits like Babe Ruth. I didn't see him until camp, and I wasn't overwhelmed. But he did have all the earmarks of a promising power prospect. He had a slight uppercut to his swing. Most left-handers with power do. In the McLaughlin faction, we were kind of joking about him, but we wouldn't have minded if it had worked out.

The club was training in Arizona and Paul asked me to check out the good young players the Cubs and the Giants had out there to see how ours compared. One day I stayed behind at the hotel to go see the Cubs while our ballclub was on the road playing an exhibition game. The telephone rang in my room, and it was the lady who managed the hotel. She said, "Mr. Russo, you're one of the coaches with the ballclub?" I said, "No, I'm a scout, I'm rooming with George Staller, he's a manager in our farm system and he's right here—is there a problem?'' She said, ''Yes, we're having problems with one of your ballplayers.'' I said, ''What's wrong?'' She said, ''He's wetting the bed every night.'' I asked who, and when I heard, I almost dropped the telephone, I was laughing so hard. When I could, I turned to Staller and said:

''George, The Babe's a bed-pisser.''

He also wasn't The Babe. Paul kept him around a while, but when his career ended he was 714 home runs short of Ruth.

Lou Kretlow was another Richards project. Paul had him with the White Sox, then brought him over to our club. We searched for reasons why and came up with one: the guy was a hell of a golfer and Paul loved to play golf. It was a factor. But not the big one.

Kretlow was a pitcher whose potential had Richards infatuated. He should have been a big winner. Some guys look like Christy Mathewson on the sidelines, but not on the mound. That was Kretlow. Nobody would ever deny he had outstanding stuff. And now and then he'd throw an outstanding game—occasionally, just enough to tease you. Paul would see one of those games and say, ''We've got to get him to do that more often.''

At his best, Kretlow would have you spellbound. You could almost see the figure 20 in front of his eyes—as in 20-game winner. And the next two or three starts, he'd get bombed. That's the difference between the mediocre ones and the good ones. The good ones will have three or four good outings, then struggle once, then start knocking off the good teams again. The mediocre guy gives you one good game, so you have faith in him for a couple of weeks, during which he's getting bombed. Then about the time you're ready to give up on him, here comes another good one. You just don't win pennants that way. The Kretlows are just good enough to get you beaten. But when all else failed, he did pay off for Richards as a golf partner.

Don't get me wrong. I like Paul, and he did build our ballclub. I thought Paul had a lot of great assets, but I also thought he let his ego get him in trouble. It hurt us as an overall organization. You need cohesion, and it wasn't possible for us to have it under those circumstances.

People called him a genius. If being eccentric is part of that, Paul qualified. He wasn't afraid to spend Baltimore's money, but he never spent much of his own. He was a well-dressed man with a reputation for spending a lot of money on clothes, but it was sort of a standing joke to watch Paul arrive at spring training. He'd bring every piece of clothing he owned and send it out to be dry cleaned, at the club's expense. He wasn't going to pay for that.

With Paul, we led the major leagues every year in, of all things, tonsillectomies. Paul was from the old school that said, "There's got to be poison in your system if you've got an injury." When our young pitchers would come up with shoulder problems, Paul would tell our team doctor, "Doc, these kids are having shoulder and arm problems. Better check those tonsils out real close." We had more kids having their tonsils removed than any other club, and it was all silly and unnecessary. The only thing wrong with those kids was they were throwing too much.

Paul and his people were obsessed with teaching. Paul envisioned himself as the greatest teacher ever, and he was a very good teacher—knowledgeable as hell, a smart man. With the White Sox before he came to us, and with our club, he had a lot of success taking worn-out pitchers and showing them another pitch, helping them become successful when it looked like their careers were shot. He called it a slip pitch, rather than a change-up. Harry Dorish, Arnie Portocarrero, Saul Rogovin, Hector "Skinny" Brown, Sandy Consuegra—people like that—were all taught the pitch by Paul.

Paul's teaching ability was genius. But he had another side that was just plain dumb. Say we're in spring training and a young kid goes three innings in an exhibition game. On most clubs, he goes out and does some running, then goes in and showers. Not on our club. We had some great young arms—Milt Pappas, Chuck Estrada, Jack Fisher, Jerry Walker—they called them "the Kiddie Korps," and that was an outstanding staff.

Freddie Hofmann was a longtime third-base coach for the Browns and then a scout for us for years. His nickname was "Boot"—short for "Boot Nose," which someone had tagged on him somewhere along the line for the broken nose that was his souvenir of playing days as a catcher for the New York Yankees (he was Babe Ruth's roommate for one season). Casey Stengel was Hofmann's good friend, and Freddie would mimic Casey talking about those arms we had: "Where the hell did you come up with those guys, Boot? Jeezus Christ, that Fisher. And Pappas. Yeah, and there's another guy there—that Aystrada. Where the hell did you get HIM?" Casey was crazy about those kids. Everybody was.

But with Paul, one of those kids would pitch in an exhibition game and, instead of running and a shower, it was to the bullpen to work on either an extra pitch or the slip pitch. And nobody's keeping track of how many pitches they're throwing. We're not talking about veterans here. We're talking about nineteen- and twenty-year-old arms. Everybody calls Paul a genius, and he was a real smart man. But how can you lose track of that?

Estrada later became a pitching coach, so he knew a little bit about the game. He told me that when he came out of a short stint in the military, Paul's staff had him throw the ball ten straight days. That's terrible. You don't do that.

So, Estrada had two good years with us and was gone at twenty-six. Walker came up at eighteen, won 11 with a 2.92 ERA at twenty, once pitched all 16 innings of a game against the White Sox, and was on his way out at twenty-two. Fisher won 12 for us at twenty-one, stayed around through the 1960s—he threw Roger Maris's 60th home run ball in 1961—but he never came back to that 1960 season with us. Pappas lasted. Oh, thank the Lord, Pappas lasted.

I really wasn't thinking too much about what was happening with the managing at that point. It was tough enough trying to walk a tightrope scouting, because of the two factions that had built up within our organization. Despite that, there was a certain amount of fun. We worked hard and had some success. Without the factions, one pulling against the other, we would have had one of the best operations going. But Paul refused to accept Jimmy McLaughlin, and Jim would not cave in to Paul. Paul couldn't fire Jimmy, even though he probably wanted to, because the owner at the time, Jim Keelty, happened to think that Jimmy was doing a hell of a job. And he was. But Paul to a lot of people was the Almighty.

The Almighty worked in strange ways. At the time he arrived in Baltimore, baseball was operating with a rule that any player who signed for more than a $4,000 bonus had to be kept on the 25-man major league roster. That's typical owners' stuff. They were bidding each other out of sight, and rather than just apply sound business practices and sign only the genuine prospects, they passed a rule that nobody could spend more than $4,000 and thought it would work—because obviously nobody wanted to let a good young talent rot on a major league bench when he could be ripening in the minor leagues.

The problem was people kept paying the big bonuses, but they'd lie about it. The money was being given out under the table, and we were as guilty as anybody. Money-laundering was not invented by Ollie North. We ran an Irangate when a lot of people were still calling that place Persia. We threw money around—almost literally.

Dutch Dietrich signed a catcher out of Oklahoma and gave him a big pile of dough under the table. He turned out to be a dog. Honest to God, he wouldn't even catch batting practice in spring training—said it was too much like work.

With our club, only one man knew what was going on under the table, and how, and that was Paul Richards. He could cheat as well as anybody, and he had friends all over the United States, so that made it easy. Say we wanted to sign a kid to big money and we couldn't allow it to be in our club's financial records; one of Paul's friends would come up with the money, in cash, and who would know?

Dutch Dietrich had the best story of all in illustrating how exotic the whole thing could get. Dutch was to pass a bundle full of cash to a guy riding on a train, without the train ever stopping. They knew what they were doing; they had done it before. The train would go through a small town in Texas real slow, the guy would reach down and get the bundle from Dutch, and the money would eventually go to a player we were cheating on. This time Dutch stumbled just as he was handing the money over, the bundle fell close to the tracks, and it broke wide open—$100 bills flying all over the place.

Kentucky basketball and Emery Air Freight in the 1980s had nothing on the Orioles of the 1950s.

But we weren't alone. I remember McLaughlin telling me one time, "I think we're all cheating, except for maybe two or three clubs." Cincinnati was one that I remember he didn't think was cheating.

But nobody would admit they were cheating, which is why there weren't more Dutch Dietrich stories. They happened, but nobody talked about them, not even in the rare times when several of us would happen to be together relaxing over a beer or two. Some subjects were just taboo. Anything that was tantamount to admitting there was some cheating going on fit into that group.

I remember one of those years, right after we had signed some pretty good kids, a guy from the Red Sox who cheated like hell got on me pretty good: "You guys are getting all these ballplayers. No damned wonder. We know what's going on. We know what you guys are doing." I took offense. I said, "You criticize all you want. But you clean the dirt out of your own kitchen first. We know what *you* guys are doing." I was pissed off.

But I didn't deny that we were cheating. We had no other choice. It was cheat or finish in last place, which would be cheating our fans as well as risking our whole business. This wasn't college. This was a fight for survival.

Paul and his coaches were always trying to change somebody, and not just pitchers. Joe Durham was hitting .391 for our San Antonio ballclub in 1957, and our big league club wasn't playing very well, so they called Durham up. He reported to the ballclub in Cleveland. He played two ballgames, and after the second game, Al Vincent, one of Paul's coaches, went up to him and said, "You're not going to hit that way. No way." And Paul agreed. "Joe, as soon as you get to Baltimore, we'll straighten some things."

The guy just finished hitting three-ninety-one.

I wasn't with the club in Cleveland, but I was in Baltimore when they came back. I walked into the ballpark and Joe Durham was in the batting cage. It's his fourth day up, and they're pitching batting practice to him—with a rope around his chest, tying him to the batting cage. They told him he was lunging. The rope was supposed to keep him from lunging, and it sure as hell did. He was tied to the cage.

I knew Joe. When no one was looking, he turned around to me and said, "Three-ninety-one and they tie a rope around my chest." It just killed him. He wasn't the same after that.

Maybe he *was* lunging. Fine. But you don't start making drastic changes after two damned ballgames. You say, "This man was tearing up the Texas League pretty good, for crying out loud. Let's look at him for a while and see what he does on his own. Maybe he can hit by lunging." Normally you can't. The pitchers will start changing up on you and get you off-stride. But you never know.

That was Paul—teach, teach, teach, twenty-four hours a day. Al Vincent was obsessed with his teaching ability. I had breakfast with Al at our hotel one morning and he was almost in tears. "Russo," he said, "if they will just listen to me, I know I can help them." He sounded like Jimmy Swaggart. I just looked at him. It was an obsession with him. There have been some pretty good hitting instructors in baseball, but he wasn't one of them.

I'm pretty sure Fred Valentine would agree with me.

Fred was one of my near-misses, a player who made it to the big league club but wasn't quite what I—and a lot of other people, including Paul Richards—thought he might be when we saw him as a prospect. And I've always felt Al Vincent had a role in Fred Valentine's falling just a little bit short.

As cold and impersonal as scouting evaluations have to be, it's a human game. With all players you sign, you like their chances to be a player—or you wouldn't be going that far. With some, you like the person inside that talent package, too—and Fred Valentine was one of the nicest people I've ever been involved with.

Fred came along before the free-agent draft. I signed him out of college, Tennessee A&I—Tennessee State now, in Nashville. I went in to see him in the spring of 1956. That was just two years after the Supreme Court's ruling that broke up school segregation, and there was some tension across the South. Tennessee A&I was all-black, and it was a funny thing—there weren't many scouts (pretty much an all-white profession then) who went onto campuses like that one in that era. I did, in checking out Fred Valentine, and it was one of the really pleasant memories I have about scouting.

Tennessee A&I came across to me in those days as more of a community, a family, than a campus. I remember walking on campus with Fred. A little girl passed us on the sidewalk and exchanged greetings with him. I said, ''Now, Fred, don't tell me that girl's in college.'' He said, ''No, she's not. But she's going to be some day, and you're going to hear about her.'' It was Wilma Rudolph, who later that year, at age sixteen, ran for the U.S. in the Olympic Games in Melbourne and then won three gold medals as a sprinter in the Rome Olympics in 1960.

Fred Valentine was more noted at Tennessee A&I as a football player than a baseball player, mainly because the football program was so good. Go back there now and you'll find the football stadium is on John Merritt Drive. John Merritt was to Tennessee A&I what Jake Gaither was to Florida A&M and what Eddie Robinson has always been to Grambling—a great football coach who stayed around a long while and had tremendous impact on his kids and his school.

It wasn't easy to pull Fred Valentine away from John Merritt's program, because Fred was a hell of a football player. When I first told Fred the Orioles were interested in him, he said, ''Mr. Russo, I want to finish school (he did—got his degree in education). And football is foremost in my mind. But baseball is big, too."

I suggested he just come to Baltimore as our guest, put on a uniform and work out. He did, and I'll tell you I never saw Paul Richards more excited. Fred stepped up and hit shots into the lower stands, and the upper stands. He's a switch-hitter, so he turns around and does the same thing the other way. I know it's just batting practice, but we've got long-time big leaguers that we haven't seen do that, and Richards is beside himself. "Oh, Jesus Christ, Mays can't even do stuff like that," Paul said. I told him, "But, Paul, I can't get him to commit himself. He doesn't know what he wants to do, baseball or football." Paul just shook his head. "This guy could be a rich man."

We flew back to Nashville and Fred was still undecided. He said, "Mr. Russo, would you be willing to talk to President Davis?" He referred to Dr. Walter S. Davis, the university president. Would I? Of course, for that one request told me two things: what a tightly knit university this was, and the standing Fred Valentine had in it. It also was an honor a baseball scout doesn't get every day—and what a nice man Dr. Davis was. He said, "Mr. Russo, I can't tell you what this young man has meant to this school. He not only is one of the finest athletes we've ever had, he's also one of the finest human beings. I think he wants to play baseball. He likes you; he likes your organization. But you have to promise me that you're going to take care of this young man." I said, "Doctor, I concur with everything you've said about him. You have my word. He'll be treated fairly." And Fred said, "OK, Mr. Russo, I'll sign."

We went from there to the hotel where I was staying. Fred said, "I can't go in that door" and started to head for another entrance. I said, "The hell you can't. I'm going to walk through that door, and you're going to go with me, because you're an Oriole now and Orioles don't go through side doors."

Fred was pretty good, one of the fastest players in our entire organization. His third year, he led the Carolina League in hitting and made the jump all the way up to Miami in the International League. That's where he ran into Al "The Silver Fox"

Vincent, who was managing the club. Fred would go to the plate and maybe strike out or ground out—he had trouble with pitchers working him tight—and he would go back to the bench and hear Vincent: "You're dead meat, Valentine. Dead meat. Jesus Christ, are you dead!" It killed me that a baseball man would talk like that, and Fred never really did make it with us. Could he have if Vincent had encouraged him instead of cutting him down? We'll never know, but he did go to Washington and had some pretty good years.

Four years after I signed Fred, I went back to Tennessee State to watch their club play and they had a good-looking ball-player, Sam Bowens. I thought we'd have a good chance of getting him, because of the relationships that built up over Fred Valentine, and I was right. All the doors were open for me to get Sam, and I did. He had a hell of a rookie year for us (22 homers and 71 RBI for our 1964 team), but Sam was altogether different from Freddie. Sam was a skirt-chaser. One morning in Milwaukee, I got up fairly early to go to breakfast and Sam was just coming in. I thought, "Oh, shit." And I was right. In fact, that was a good description of Sam after that rookie year.

Paul Richards was gone from us by the time Sam came up. The club took away half of Paul's job by bringing Lee MacPhail in as general manager in 1958 and smoothing out the intra-organizational strife. Then, on Sept. 1, 1961, after the flirtation with success in 1960, but with the "Kiddie Korps" already starting to come apart, Paul resigned as manager and his long-time friend and coach, Luman Harris, filled out that year.

As I said, Paul was eccentric and egocentric and every other -centric you could imagine, but his era was a big, big plus for the Orioles. He took over a 54-100 club and left with a 95-67 team, good enough to win in a lot of years but not in "The Year of Maris and Mantle" and the 1961 Yankees. Our best record ever left us 14 games out.

6

The Man Who Made the Difference

Draft day in pro football has become the fans' most electrifying day. Bigger to the broad spectrum of fans than the Super Bowl, because only two teams' fans are involved there. Bigger than the first day of the season, because football never has and never will equal baseball's opening-day charm (can you imagine politicians falling all over themselves to make the first kickoff?). Draft day is ahead of everything for fans, because it's the day dreaming is legal, and almost rational.

June 15 used to be that kind of day in baseball.

That was the trading deadline.

Fans live for trades. Yet, they're the world's worst traders. All they want to do is help their own club, which is exactly what motivates any general manager who sits down to talk trade. But that general manager is sitting across from—or on the other end of a telephone line with—another general manager with the same desires, so the understanding comes quite quickly that you indeed do have to give something to get something.

It's amazing how that never has sunk in for some of the greatest, most passionate, seemingly most knowledgeable fans in the world. Certainly, it hasn't occurred to the ones who frequent those modern-day radio staples, the call-in talk shows.

Let's say it's St. Louis.

(Caller) "I've got a trade."

(Host) "OK, let's hear it."

"We need a hitter. Let's get Cal Ripken."

"Who would you give up?"

"Well, if we had Ripken, we could give up Jose Oquendo. And Tim Jones. So give them Oquendo and Jones—and maybe one other guy. Milt Thompson?"

That's just not the way things get done in real trading. To begin with, you don't insult the intelligence of the man across the table by even bringing up the name of a talent like a Ripken. And if he's available, you'd have to back off a minute and wonder why.

I don't mean to just blow off call-in shows. Some fans, and some hosts, come up with ideas that aren't bad. I remember in my latter years with the Orioles, Randy Galloway, a baseball writer for the *Dallas Morning News* and a talk-show host, told me the Orioles were crazy for not trading with the Rangers to get Charlie Hough. "He beats the hell out of you guys," Randy said. "If you had him, you wouldn't have to face him." It wasn't bad advice, but we didn't follow up on it. And he was still beating us into the 1990s.

For the most part on call-in shows, though, a high percentage of the fans calling in with ideas operate with beautifully one-dimensional vision: What do *we* need?

Believe it or not, there are general managers just like that. They don't make many trades, and they don't understand why not.

But some trades are made, and they're always headline news. That's the grip baseball has on America. If two teams make a trade involving starting players, and it's December 9, it will get big play in Keokuk, Iowa. Baseball is a year-round game, with two seasons: in-season and off-season. And trades excite people in both.

It is politic to say the best trades help both teams. The

theory is good: If, a year or two later, the fellow on the other end is as pleased with what you gave him as you are with what he gave you, the foundation of trust is there for further business. So that's what you should always shoot for—two happy parties.

Right. Just like you always hope the used car dealer sitting across the desk from you will wind up as happy as you. You're *hoping* to unload the flaws that made you deal in the first place and come up with a jewel that will be flawless when you get it and get better as time goes on.

There's a little used car dealer in all of us when we sit down to trade.

There's some gambler, too. It's you, the scout, whose chin is out, because scouts' judgments make the difference in trades. The general manager makes the deal, but he is going on what his major league scout tells him regarding the ability of the players involved. Make enough deals and you're bound to be burned badly at times. You're graded on how many more times you're the burner than the burnee, and the grade may not come in for three or four years.

When the Yankees traded Fred McGriff to Toronto in 1982, he was strictly a throw-in, the kind of name that fills out a lot of trades and never surfaces in print again. McGriff was an eighteen-year-old kid who had hit .272 with 9 home runs in his second time around at Bradenton, in the lowest level of minor league ball, a rookie league. The key player in that deal was relief pitcher Dale Murray. The Yankees just had to have him—so much that they were willing to give up Dave Collins, who was a pretty good outfielder at the time; Mike Morgan, who bounced around some (including an undistinguished stop with our organization) before a fair year with the Dodgers in 1991 got him a big contract with the Cubs...

And McGriff. *Plus $400,000.*

For all of that they got Murray and Tom Dodd (for the record, not the one who was a senator from Connecticut—and, as it turned out, not a prospect, either).

It wasn't until five years later that McGriff even surfaced

with Toronto, but a year after that he was a star. Meanwhile, Murray, the whole reason for the trade, had two poor years with the Yankees and then was released, the end of a good career that unfortunately for the poor guy's baseball memory included a key role as a disappointment in another major trade: he and Woodie Fryman from Montreal to Cincinnati for Tony Perez and Will McEnaney. That wintertime trade after the 1976 World Series is the one Reds fans always will pinpoint as the start of the Big Red Machine's disintegration. And they're probably right. Perez was not only popular because he was just a remarkable clutch player, good enough that one day he'll be in Cooperstown, but he also was a binding agent on a team of superstars. The club never was the same after Perez left, and Murray didn't help because he came in with the pressure on him and totally fizzled. That happens, but what makes his situation different is that he was so good in the other parts of his career that *two* clubs got stung trading for him.

The key word for me in all of that is Cincinnati. Every time I hear the words ''Cincinnati'' and ''trade,'' I break out in a wide smile.

No deal in all my years in baseball had the impact of the one that sent Frank Robinson from Cincinnati to Baltimore in 1965. Apparently I'm not the only one who feels that way. In the summer of 1988, Edmonton almost touched off a Canadian revolt by sending Wayne Gretzky to Los Angeles in a deal that involved four other players, three No. 1 draft picks and 10 million dollars. Associated Press accompanied the Gretzky trade story with a list of the ''blockbuster'' trades in sports history, and it tickled me to see that the only genuine baseball trade (four men, no cash) on the list was the one we made with Cincinnati on Dec. 9, 1965: Robinson to us for pitchers Milt Pappas and Jack Baldschun and outfielder Dick Simpson.

Let me tell you how that trade happened.

The Orioles actually became a winner in 1964. That was the year the White Sox swept four games from the Yankees in Chicago in mid-August and left 'em for dead. On the way to O'Hare airport after that series is when Phil Linz played a harmonica on the team bus and Yogi Berra, in his first year as manager, blew skyhigh, as a lot of other competitors I've known would have. There are times when silence is not only golden but damned near mandatory, and a bus trip after a four-game sweep is certainly one of those.

We followed the Yankees into Chicago that weekend and our young third baseman, Brooks Robinson, beat them with his bat three games in a row. All of a sudden, we were the team out front heading for the wire. But guess who got there first? The Yankees made one of their deadline waiver deals to pick up Pedro Ramos, a fair pitcher but nothing better than that up to then, his only distinction prior to that being the fact that he led the league in losses four straight years—the only guy who ever did that. The Yankees had won other pennants by getting Johnny Mize, Johnny Hopp, Enos Slaughter, Johnny Sain—guys like that just in time to be eligible for the World Series, but I remember thinking if Ramos was the best they could do this time, we're all right. He went into the Yankee bullpen and was absolutely unhittable the rest of the way. The Yankees won 10 straight and 26 out of 32, and we finished third—2 games behind New York, 1 behind Chicago, even though we won 97 games.

The only trinket we took away from that little experience was the league MVP award for Brooks Robinson, his introduction, at twenty-seven, to real stardom. That was nice, but not very satisfying, and we looked to 1965 with anticipation because we knew the Yankees were headed down and we were young and rising. Our pitching staff that year was the "Baby Birds"— Wally Bunker, nineteen (19-5), Dave McNally, twenty-one (9-11), Steve Barber, twenty-five (9-13) and the ace, Milt Pappas, twenty-five (16-7).

The next year the Yankees' era was over, just as we suspected. But Minnesota was the American League champion, and we were third again—eight games out this time. We knew we couldn't stand pat.

Meanwhile, Cincinnati, which had won the National League pennant in 1961 with Frank Robinson as MVP, also had gone to the final day in 1964 with a chance to win and then skidded off to fourth in 1965. The star of 1961, Robinson, still was producing big numbers (33 home runs, 113 RBI), but he had just turned thirty—an "old thirty," one of the Reds' officials put it—and he was making $68,700 a year, more than Bill DeWitt (my old boss, who had switched leagues) wanted to pay anybody. Frank also had made the mistake, in an old and conservative town, of being picked up by police at a late-night restaurant with a gun in his possession. A "bad actor" rap started to build, and not just in Cincinnati.

At the winter meetings that year, Cincinnati was shopping Frank Robinson, but not openly. Jim McLaughlin—who had left the Orioles to join DeWitt with the Reds—handed me a note and said, "Take this to your people." The note said: "Pappas, Baldschun and Blefary for F. Robinson." I was stunned. I had no idea a player that good would be available, but I went running with that note and figured I would have no difficulty selling the trade.

Our manager, Hank Bauer, was dead-set against making that trade. "You're asking me to give up my best pitcher," Hank kept saying. We were, of course, bringing along an awfully good looking young kid in Jim Palmer. But he was barely twenty years old then and neither I nor anyone else could say with any conviction that he was ready to step in and replace Pappas. I liked Pappas, but I argued like hell to make the trade.

And I got no help. Jerry Hoffberger, our owner, and vice president Frank Cashen were in the room, but they stayed in the corner and did not interfere. I'm sure Hoffberger felt he was doing the right thing, letting baseball people decide baseball matters. That's what he was paying us for. So he just sat back and listened—and so did Cashen, who was (and is) a good baseball man—to Bauer, Harry Dalton, Billy Hunter and me.

Finally, when nobody else challenged Bauer, I got mad. I walked over to Cashen and Hoffberger, looked them in the eye and said, "If we don't make this deal, we'll be making one of the biggest mistakes we'll ever make. I've seen this guy in the National League. I *know* what he can do." They just listened, and wouldn't intervene.

The thing that eventually held it up was not Pappas. The Reds also wanted Curt Blefary and we drew the line there. I was in favor of the deal, in spite of Blefary, but I went along: if the consensus was that we wouldn't part with Blefary, we wouldn't. And it was, so we didn't. The Orioles, on the field or in the front office, believed in team work.

Now, granted, in hindsight we don't look very bright on that. Curt Blefary never in his baseball life was worth jeopardizing a Frank Robinson trade, but funny things come into play when you're making a trade. Blefary was the American League Rookie of the Year that year. You just don't trade the Rookie of the Year the year after he wins it, because if you do you're going to catch hell from a lot of people and lose some numbers at the gate. And don't believe for a minute that the thought of hot press and public criticism and declining attendance doesn't scare the boldest trader.

We were a damned sight short of bold on this one. We didn't know how good Blefary was going to be, but we all—me included—thought he would be all right, not great but good. We sat down and contemplated everything and said, ''We can't do it with Blefary in the deal.''

So the meetings are over and I'm flying back to St. Louis. It just happens that on the flight I sit beside Herk Robinson, the assistant farm director for Cincinnati then. The hostess brought us a drink and we're sitting there chatting. He said, ''It looks like our deal is dead, huh?'' I said, ''I think so, Herk, as long as you people keep insisting on Curt Blefary. He was just voted Rookie of the Year. We're a young organization. They might run us out of town.''

Herk nodded and didn't say anything. After a few minutes, he said, ''You guys acquired Simpson today, didn't you?'' Dick Simpson was a twenty-two-year-old outfielder in the California Angels' system. We picked him up in a minor deal for Norm Siebern, who had been a good player but was thirty-two and just about done. Simpson had hit .301 in the Pacific Coast League with 24 home runs and looked like a prospect. Obviously, we had beaten the Reds to him.

"Would you be interested in talking about Simpson, rather than Blefary?" I said.

"We certainly would," Herk said. "Our Triple-A manager [Dave Bristol, who was managing San Diego] likes Simpson very much."

I said, "Well, why don't you call Bill DeWitt when you get into St. Louis and I'll call our people, but I can tell you now we would be receptive to that. You can take my word on that."

He got really excited. He called DeWitt from the airport. He didn't even wait till he got home. Lee MacPhail had just left our front office to become American League president, and Harry Dalton was brand new on the job as our player personnel director. While Herk was calling DeWitt, I was on the phone with Harry. He asked me, "Would you do that?" I said, "Harry, if we don't do that, we don't deserve to win another ballgame."

Harry said, "Yeah, but Robinson's reputation..." I said, "Forget about his reputation. Forget about everything. Just call DeWitt and make the God-damned deal."

Harry made the call, and then he started getting cute. This is Harry's first experience with negotiations. He calls DeWitt to close the deal, and at the last minute he's trying to get another ballplayer from the Reds. DeWitt was shrewd, one of the best traders I've ever been associated with, smart as hell when it came to making a deal. He said, "Harrrryyyy, you're just about to screw up a million-dollar deal. I'm not going to play games with you." Dalton got smart and quit trying to be cute. We made the trade: Pappas, Simpson and another pitcher named Jack Baldschun for Robinson.

Harry always had that tendency, trying to extract that extra player at the last minute. There may be a time and a place for that stuff, but in a deal like this—what if DeWitt had had another trade working for Frank? We might have lost the guy because Harry was trying to get another player.

We would never have known what we missed, because we got awfully good awfully fast when Frank arrived. You can have a real, real good ballclub and maybe not win because you don't know exactly how to win. I think that was as much of our problem in 1964 as that damned Pedro Ramos was.

Frank Robinson, I think, showed us how to win, or taught us, by the way he played the game—for keeps. We had a good ballclub all along. Frank put intangibles to work. For all of his home runs and clutch hits, the play that best exemplified Frank Robinson to me came in Game 6 of the 1971 World Series. We're down 3 games to 2, and Frank is on first base with one out in the bottom of the tenth inning of a 2-2 game. He's hurting—legs gimpy from the strain of the season, one Achilles tendon really sore. Merv Rettenmund punched a single to center, and Frank dared the Pirates to throw him out at third. His head-first dive just did get him in safely, and he scored the winning run on Brooks Robinson's short fly ball. He could have looked foolish, in a circumstance like that, but he knew his ability well enough to bet on it, and won us a game. When a sore, thirty-five-year-old superstar hustles in the clutch like that, everybody else on the ballclub gets a little bit better, a little more determined, a little less likely to give anything less than 100 percent effort. That's what I mean about putting intangibles—not to mention wonderful baseball instincts—to work in a winning way.

The minute Frank crossed the white line he became a vicious son of a gun. They knocked him down, he got right up. He became our leader. His first year with us he won the Triple Crown: 49 home runs, 122 RBI, .316. We were good for Frank, when you stop and consider his problems, but I'm going to tell you he was good for us, too. I feel we showed him what a class organization was. But he also showed us a lot of things that we weren't aware of.

He was the greatest clutch hitter I've ever seen—better than Mantle, better than Mays, better than Aaron. And that's saying it as strongly as I can because those other three also were genuinely great players. In that specific area—delivering in the clutch, somehow, some way—I rank Frank No. 1.

The other great example, of course, was that first time he came up in the 1966 World Series. We had won the pennant by eight games that year. Now we're going into the World Series, first time ever, and we're up against the Dodgers, who have won it twice in the last three years and have Sandy Koufax and Don Drysdale as the living legends of that time. Now, the Series starts, and everybody's uptight. And what does Robinson do? First time up, against Drysdale, two-run homer. You could feel the weight just being lifted off everybody's shoulders, especially after Brooks followed Frank's homer with another one. Both of those guys were home run hitters who hit them when they *really* meant something.

That season with Frank Robinson was an experience for me, and I'm sure for our ballclub. This is the point I was trying to get across when Hank Bauer was telling me, "You're asking me to give up my best pitcher." To this day, Frank Cashen and I will discuss it and, oh, Frank gets upset—because Bauer will take credit for making the deal. Frank will say to me, "Why does he want to lie like that?" I'll say, "Hank's that kind of guy. You think he's going to tell people that he didn't want any part of Frank Robinson because he didn't want to have to give up Milt Pappas?"

7

The Cooperstown Kids

As vital as Frank Robinson was in putting us over the top, the player who led us into contention was Brooks Robinson, though his greatest fame wasn't to come until later.

In many ways, Brooks is still the ultimate Oriole: quiet, dependable, out there every day.

And great.

There again is that word I don't like to use. If I can't use it for the Brooks Robinson I saw redesign the fine art of playing third base, I won't ever use it. Nobody equaled him. Nobody approached him.

More than that, he was our building block. We formed a team around him, because when he joined us, we were, very frankly, a baseball joke.

Oh, we had been worse. We were the Orioles, at least, not the lowly, miserable, financially strapped Browns by the time Brooks signed with us in Little Rock, Arkansas, at eighteen years of age in the spring of 1955.

Maybe my favorite story showing just how tough things got with the Browns came in 1950, when Zack Taylor was managing the team, and finishing last or next-to-last every year.

The Yankees used to just tear the Browns apart. It was piti-ful. Zack took his 1950 ballclub into Yankee Stadium for the first time. His players were all sitting in the clubhouse, most of them facing the lockers, not even facing Zack. But he gave them a fire-up speech, anyway.

"OK, men," Zack said, "we're playing the Yankees.

"I don't want any mistakes.

"Hit the cutoff man at all times.

"Don't throw the ball behind the runner.

"Run everything out.

"Let's go out there today...and look good losing."

Honest to God, that's what he said. Or honest to Billy DeMars, anyway. Billy, a minor league manager for us, was Tay-lor's shortstop on that 1950 team, and he swore those were his exact words.

The change of cities and uniforms in 1954 didn't make us good. That first season in Baltimore we finished 57 games out of first place. We won only 54 games. I think that means the league champion that year (Cleveland) had won more games by July 4 than we did playing the whole year. That's the organization young Brooks Robinson voluntarily chose to join, in the years when there was no draft to reduce players' options.

If I came across as a little harsh on Paul Richards in earlier chapters, let me give him supreme status in Orioles' fans eyes with one comment:

Paul Richards got us Brooks Robinson.

Paul had a lot of guys working on landing Brooks, but the one who went down to Little Rock and clinched it for us was Arthur Ehlers. Arthur had been general manager of the Phila-delphia A's, and he was our general manager in 1954. And Lind-say Deal, a former player under Paul, also helped immensely.

I never saw Brooks play before we signed him. They didn't even have high school baseball in Little Rock then, but I had heard of Brooks. A fan wrote me a letter about him, when he was playing American Legion ball. I mentioned the letter to Jim McLaughlin, my boss, and he said they already knew about him. Most clubs in baseball did. Like Dave McNally's, Brooks' Legion performances were well known among scouts. Some clubs thought he was a little too slow, but Paul didn't buy that. He stuck with it, and he had so many connections in baseball that he was getting really good information on Brooks—who would call the shots, important things like that.

Make no mistake. This was one of those deals where we had to cheat a little. But, Paul handled that about as well as it could have been handled.

Still, Arthur Ehlers put the clincher on. Orioles fans can remember him with a little special reverence, too.

Brooks played his first games as an Oriole that very first pro summer, when he was still eighteen. He put in 95 games in the Piedmont League with York, Pennsylvania, hit .331, and joined us for the last six games of the season. It wasn't the Brooks Robinson we grew to know. This one had as many errors in those six games as hits (two of each).

He came up at the end of the next two years, too. He stayed with us the full 1958 season and hit .238. He spent the winter in the army, but was out in time to start the season with our club. It was decided he needed work, so he was sent to Vancouver on May 5 to play his way into shape and returned July 8. That's when he was given the third base job—forever, on any all-time Baltimore team.

We spent so much time over the next decade or so admiring Brook's glove that we tended to take for granted how good he was with the bat. In the clutch, he was exceptional, *very* good. When we made our unsuccessful run in 1964, Brooks led the league with 118 RBI and was the American League's MVP, one of the rare times that award didn't go to a member of the pennant-winning team.

There's a story to almost every baseball signing, especially those that came before the draft. Begun in 1965, the draft eliminated the bidding wars. I'm sure it saved baseball a lot of money, but it sure took a lot of the fun out of seeking and finding and then wooing the top prospects. Since the draft went in, only one club can make an offer to any drafted player.

It happened that way at least once before the draft, too. We got Boog Powell all to ourselves because of a coin toss—an honest-to-God flip of a coin, a story that to my knowledge never has been told.

In the spring of 1959, John Wesley Powell, a blond young giant from Key West, Florida, was being scouted and courted by every club in baseball. I knew we were in it for the distance—we even went so far as to get our owner at the time, Jim Keelty, involved. And I suspected from the start our chief opposition would come from the St. Louis Cards, because scout Whitey Reis of the Cards was very close to the Powell family.

When Powell and Key West played in the Florida state high school tournament in Fort Pierce, Florida, thirty-eight big league scouts and club officials were there. Whether that was a factor or not, Powell had a terrible tourney: one hit, a softly hit ground single through the middle. Most of the scouts couldn't wait to leave town.

That's a phenomenon I saw a lot of times and never could fathom: liking a kid for weeks or months, even years, and then dropping him when he has a bad game or tournament. But it does happen. After all that pre-tournament interest, only about four clubs remained and made appointments to talk to the Powells, and the only ones still serious about bidding for Boog were the Cards and us. We were ready to go $60,000 to $75,000 and I'm sure the Cards would have topped that. But neither of us wanted a bidding contest, and Jim McLaughlin took advantage of that with a coup I would never have thought of.

Jim called Walter Shannon, the Cardinals' farm director and a tough competitor who was there along with Reis, and asked for a meeting. In it, we discussed the situation we were both facing, and Jim said, "To avoid a bidding contest, let's flip a coin and the loser withdraws from the case, leaving Powell to the winner." I couldn't believe he did it, and I was more surprised when Shannon fell for it. Reis flipped the coin and I called tails.

It was short and sweet—and tails. The Cards shook hands and withdrew. We were in.

Almost.

We made an 11 P.M. appointment with the Powells, so we could catch them before they left Fort Pierce. As the only club left, we were pretty specific in our strategy: Bring some liquid refreshments along, chitchat a while, then after about an hour Fred Hofmann of our scouting staff was to say, ''Well, Boog, all the other clubs have deserted you, but the Orioles are still here. They still believe in you.'' Then McLaughlin fired our opening bonus offer, $25,000.

The Powells were not receptive. It was now around 1 A.M. and we were getting nowhere. We wished the Powells well and returned to our rooms at the motel, grousing all the way. It's human nature; you sense you have lost or are losing a player, and you begin to downgrade him in your mind and belittle his ability. What that told me was the refreshments were having more of an effect on McLaughlin and Hofmann than on the Powells.

McLaughlin and Hofmann went to bed. I told them I was going to take a walk before turning in. I went back by the Powells' room. By now it was 2 A.M., and everybody was asleep except for Boog's dad. The two of us sat down for a quiet talk. I went over step-by-step exactly what could and might happen in Boog's baseball career: that it was rare but conceivable that Boog could be wearing an Oriole uniform by the coming season. I told him we would start Boog in the rookie league where almost all high school signees start, and I promised we would invite him to spring training with the Orioles the following year.

It was now 4 A.M. Mr. Powell got Boog out of bed (what an awesome sight he was at four in the morning) and told him, ''I want you to listen to what Mr. Russo has to say.'' I repeated to Boog what I had promised his dad and told them to give it serious thought. It was now 5 A.M., and I told Mr. Powell I wanted an answer by 9 A.M.

I returned to my room and went to bed. At a quarter to nine, the Powells knocked on my door. They had accepted our offer for $25,000 and were ready to sign a contract.

I felt like buying Walter Shannon dinner. Many dinners. Boog bought me a lot of them by hitting 303 home runs before he wore a major league uniform other than the Orioles'.

The whole Boog Powell coin-tossing experience taught me some things, and it taught the Powells more. They knew the poor tournament performance had cost Boog big bucks. Two years later, Carl Taylor, Boog's half-brother, was a top prospect, and, needless to say, he was not permitted to play in the tournament. The Pirates signed him, but I'll bet it cost them a lot more than Boog Powell cost us, and we got 299 more home runs out of Boog than they got out of Carl Taylor.

A few years later, in 1962, Dave Johnson was a nineteen-year-old sophomore shortstop at Texas A&M. Our southwestern scout, Dee Phillips, saw him play a couple of games and told me by phone that I should see Johnson as soon as possible. I knew Dee; I flew into Fort Worth immediately to watch A&M in a game against TCU.

One look was enough for me. I was so impressed that I got on the telephone at the airport, tracked Phillips down, and told him to forget about running all over the Southwest—''keep a close eye on Johnson, see as many games as you can, stay in close personal touch.''

The general thinking was that Johnson was going to stay in school. The Orioles sponsored a team in Winner, South Dakota, in the collegiate summer Basin League, and I told Phillips to try to get Johnson signed for Winner, to strengthen our ties with him in case he turned pro the next year. When the Texas A&M season ended and Phillips talked to him about Winner, Johnson said he had decided to turn professional and forgo his final two years at A&M. That was the ''close personal touch'' I had in mind. Phillips called me immediately with the news that not only was Johnson going pro but also that he planned to fly to the Coast that week.

To me, that meant he was going to work out for the Giants and the Dodgers, who were bound to be as impressed as I was—and he'd never get away out there without signing. I felt pretty sure we wouldn't even get to make our pitch if he went to the Coast. It turned out I was a midwesterner unfamiliar with talking Texan. What Johnson was talking about doing was taking a little break and going to the *Gulf* Coast, around Corpus Christi, for some beach time. Sometimes even misinformation is a great motivator. We went to work, fast.

It was morning in St. Louis. I told Phillips to make an 11 P.M. appointment that night at the Johnsons' home in San Antonio and I would be there. I got there not knowing if any other club knew what Dee Phillips did, and after a few minutes of conversation with Dave and his parents, I was relieved. Dave had not even told his coach, Tom Chandler.

We explained to the Johnsons that we had good pitching in the Oriole organization but lacked good infielders and good hitting, so he should not have to spend too much time in the minors. They wanted to know where he would go. I told them we had a spot waiting for him with our Stockton club in the Class C California State League, the best C league in the country then and equivalent to Class A now. I assured him he would play every day. He appeared interested.

It was nearing 1 A.M. I asked him what he had in mind regarding money. Without hesitation, he said a $40,000 bonus, a reasonable salary, and payment for the remainder of his schooling at a school of his choosing. I wouldn't have blinked at $100,000, so naturally I said, "We'll accept that." Dee had brought along a contract, already prepared except for the figures, so I filled in the amount and gave it to Dave for his and his father's signature.

Before he signed, Johnson said he wanted to call his coach. I shocked him. "No, Dave, I can't allow that." He became adamant, and I didn't back down. Here I am, in his own home, in the presence of his parents—his dad was a retired Army colonel, no country bumpkin—telling him he couldn't make a call to his coach, or even use his own phone! I said if he insisted, we would be forced to withdraw our offer. They found that hard to comprehend, and I wasn't totally sure about the strategy myself. I knew I was taking a hell of a risk that could have cost us one of the best players we ever had, one I badly wanted to sign.

At about 2 A.M., Johnson signed the contract, along with his father.

"Now," he said, "why wouldn't you let me call Coach Chandler?"

"Because," I told him, "Your coach is on the Houston payroll, to recommend players." And he was. I was certain if he had received that late-night telephone call, Chandler would have advised Dave to hold off—and then contacted Houston. And the Houston club was spending a lot of money in those days.

The next day, Chandler—who was and is a good friend of mine—called a press conference and said the Baltimore Orioles and Jim Russo had cost Texas A&M the next two Southwest Conference championships. That made me mad. I called a press conference myself and said it was solely Johnson's decision to turn professional and that the Orioles' big concern was being fair to Johnson, not to Texas A&M. I said we would pay for the remainder of Johnson's education, which we paid for in full. I never asked a kid to give up a college scholarship unless I could guarantee him his education, and at one time the Orioles were paying college expenses for fifty-four players in the organization. Johnson got his degree—at Trinity University in San Antonio.

And the Orioles got a hell of a second baseman.

Another key signee was Wally Bunker. Don McShane was our West Coast scout who deserves all the credit on that one.

Don had a tough job, evaluating California kids. Bunker threw hard, with good breaking stuff. And he always had real good poise.

That tended to be typical of California ballplayers. They matured earlier than midwestern and eastern kids because of the chance to play year-round. At that time, some colleges in California would play 100 games while northern colleges were lucky to get in 20. You had to take that into consideration in scouting.

With the California kid: "Has he reached his level? Is he going to get any better than this?"

Wally Bunker was good to begin with. He played only half a season in the minors before coming up to the Orioles while still eighteen. He was 19-5 in the major leagues when he was only nineteen. So when we asked the California question about him, the answer was, "Maybe he won't be getting any better, but where he is right now isn't bad."

The line in the baseball record books says: "Received reported $40,000 bonus to sign with Baltimore Orioles, 1963."

That's precise and accurate wording.

That *was* the reported figure.

A scout can spend a lifetime waiting to see a Jim Palmer.

Jim Wilson, the scout who had been so excited about Dave McNally a few years before, was the first one in our organization to check out Palmer as an Arizona high school youngster in 1963. At that time, the view on him was mixed. Some scouts loved him, and some were only mildly interested.

Jim Wilson liked him so much he asked me to put him on our summertime club in Winner, South Dakota. We had an opening, but what Wilson was asking was highly unusual, if not unprecedented. The league was very competitive for college players; it wasn't for high school players. Wilson said, "Don't worry. Palmer will hold his own." So, I called Harry Wise (the manager there and a good high school coach in Englewood, Colorado) and told him we were sending Palmer along. Harry didn't have much choice but I'm sure he wasn't ecstatic. It wasn't very long before Wise, a former pitcher, was calling us himself, *really* high on Palmer. And this was in a summer when Harry's staff also included Jim Lonborg, who became an outstanding pitcher for the Red Sox. In fact, he had just a hell of a club overall, one I was in charge of supplying and very proud of. The seventeen guys on that team *all* signed professional contracts. I don't know of another situation where that ever happened. Bobby Floyd and

Merv Rettenmund from that club made it to the big leagues, in addition to Palmer and Lonborg.

I visited the club in August for one week and saw Palmer pitch a night game. That was one of those nights I had in mind when I told my scouts there would be times when the prospect was so good, you not only saw him with your eyes, you felt him in your heart. Palmer was so good he gave me chills.

I sat there and marveled. I had never seen such poise or a fastball that live in a young kid. He had a no-hitter until the right-fielder messed up. Even that didn't ruffle him, although I've seen something like that throw off a veteran pitcher. All night long, I sat there looking at the same, smooth delivery he had throughout his career.

I couldn't do anything to sign him there. Baseball rules of the time prohibited the signing of those players until the season was over, and I knew Jim had plans to go to Arizona State, which would put him out of my reach under a different baseball rule. Here, too, there were violations. I've always felt the reason I didn't get Lonborg was that the Red Sox signed him during the season. I had a good relationship with Jim, but whenever I talked to him that summer in Winner, he gave me a look that told me he was hiding something. One day, I came straight out: ''Tell me how much you want—we'll give you whatever you want.'' He still didn't answer me. That told me he already was committed to Boston.

So, Palmer had my total concentration, and after confirming my extremely high opinion of him with that August drop-in, I had to leave—no easy feat in Winner. The closest commercial airport was 160 miles away in Sioux Falls, so I asked Harry Wise to have someone drive me there—someone named Jim Palmer.

It gave me a great opportunity to learn more about Jim and to try to sell him on the Orioles organization. He said he did plan to enter Arizona State in the fall. I couldn't argue strongly against that; Arizona State had a hell of a program. I just told Jim if that was what he did, we sure wanted to keep in touch with him and he could count on being invited back to Winner the next summer. Those minutes with him in that car underlined even more strongly to me that what we were dealing with here was a very mature eighteen-year-old.

A few days after the Basin League season ended, I got a call from Jim Wilson: "Jim Palmer has decided to sign now and go to college in the off-season." My heart had no time for even a flicker of remorse for Arizona State; it was beating too fast with excitement for the Orioles. I told Wilson to make an appointment with Palmer the next day in Scottsdale, and I'd be there.

Wilson and I walked into the Palmer home and saw the reason for the sudden change of mind. There sat the pitcher of our dreams with his right knee wrapped, swollen sickeningly, a crutch beside him for when he dared to try to walk. Palmer had driven home from Winner with another player, and they were involved in an accident that could have been worse. Their car flipped over, and Jim had torn knee cartilage.

I wasn't prepared for that sight. My whole game plan was dashed. All I could think was: "How bad is this? Will he ever pitch again? Will his fastball be gone?" I had some decisions to make, fast.

The first one I made was that the front office wasn't going to hear about this from me. Harry Dalton was the Orioles farm director, and I knew he would nix the deal. I had taken him into Winner once, but he saw Palmer pitch just one inning and left noncommittal. In a true sense, he hadn't *seen* that grace, that fastball—or for damned sure that knee. I had seen all three, and I wasn't going to let someone else decide that the last one meant more than the first two. I read one time that a college basketball recruiter named Dave Pritchett said: "There's a beautiful woman on every street corner in America, but a shot-blocking big man is hard to find." So is that grace, that fastball.

The Palmers told me their family doctor already had told them Jim would need surgery. I didn't know the doctor, but I knew how valuable that knee was. I stressed to the Palmers that they should make sure they were getting the best orthopedic surgeon in the Phoenix area—and to do it all quietly.

Prior to arriving in Phoenix, I had called Baltimore to check on the bonus limits, and the word was different from what I had heard with McNally. Money is short, our new general manager, Lee MacPhail, told me, and he was excited about a hell of a ballplayer right there in the Baltimore area ready to sign, a kid named Ron Swoboda. "This kid is local," I was told. "We *have* to sign him."

I was furious, but I was talking to my boss. I told MacPhail if we lost Palmer, we were losing one of the best young pitchers I had ever seen. I pleaded with him: "If Swoboda is that good, Lee, we've got to sign them both. But we *can't* lose Palmer." He told me we were paying attention to budgets now, and the money that we had left said we could sign just one of the two: Palmer or Swoboda. He left no doubt that he felt the hometown kid should come first.

I went to Phoenix with that hanging over me, but when I called back to the office after arriving, I was told that Swoboda had decided to enter the University of Maryland. The Terps could have tapped me for a pretty good donation at that moment. I've kinda liked Maryland teams ever since.

So, with a sigh of relief, Wilson and I stayed with our evening appointment with the Palmers. We were on the eight o'clock shift. The Houston Astros and their new manager, a fellow named Paul Richards, were on at six.

We had a nice meeting with the Palmers—Jim; his parents, Max and Polly, without doubt two of the nicest people I've ever met; Jim's fiancee, Susan Ryan; and Jim's eighteen-year-old sister. The meeting got nicer in my view when it became apparent that Paul Richards had failed to impress the Palmers. I don't know if Paul was a little turned off by the sight of that swollen knee or not, but he came across to the Palmers as high-handed and ill-mannered. Right in the midst of talking to the Palmers, Paul got up, picked up a golf putter and practiced putting in the middle of the room—talking through it all. He told them he would take Jim in tow and personally work with him, but it was obvious that a lot of that "personally" stuff lost its punch when the guy making the statement was talking rather abstractly, his eyes fixed on a putter and a golf ball, not on the eyes of the person he was trying to sell.

When he stopped his putting long enough to tell Jim's sister to go get him a glass of water, it was all over. The water he got wasn't the only thing that was chilled by then.

The Palmers told us all these things, and we were perfect gentlemen. We could afford to be. We just smiled and said nothing, just gave a little sympathetic, well-timed shake of the head every now and then. Paul's performance made us look like the most charming guys ever to enter a home, before we said a word.

We didn't have to say as much as usual. I already had made Jim familiar with the Orioles organization, on that drive to the airport. Wilson had met the parents. He and the Palmers had a warm enough relationship that fairly quickly we got to the key question: What kind of bonus are you expecting? Knee injury or no knee injury, they came back with what they thought was top dollar for the time: $40,000.

They were about right. That's the figure that sportswriters had been estimating in the newspapers when other top prospects that summer had signed, so the Palmers accepted it as the going rate. It wasn't a bad figure for then.

I said if that was agreeable with them, it was with us—and we would throw in a guarantee to pay for Jim's college education at the school of his choice, so giving up the Arizona State scholarship wasn't costing him anything.

Polly Palmer liked that, as any mother would, and she made one additional request: a new Chevy Sting Ray—I was never sure whether it was for her or for Jim. I didn't let it get far enough to know. Much as I hated to inject anything negative into a conversation that was going beautifully, I said rather firmly and bluntly: "No. That's impossible. The Baltimore Orioles don't give cars."

And I meant it. Scouting and law have one thing in common: once something becomes precedent, it's repeated. If the newspapers had printed that we gave a prospect a car, every kid would have been wanting one when he signed. I could have won Jim Palmer and lost my job. Boy, I loved Jim Palmer, but not that much.

Thank God it never came to that. Once the car request was rejected, the subject never came up again. Jim signed, we had a Hall of Famer, and I still had my job. Damned if I didn't think I was pretty good at it, too, that night—and on the day just a little more than two years later when twenty-year-old Jim Palmer beat Sandy Koufax in the World Series.

The first weekend in August of 1990 brought the Jim Palmer baseball story to a wonderful ending—certainly for him, but for an awful lot of other people, too, including me. Jim Palmer, boy wonder of not quite a quarter-century past, was taken into the Baseball Hall of Fame at Cooperstown.

Only the game's true elite get there, and Jim—and Joe Morgan, the classy little second baseman from that Cincinnati "Big Red Machine" of the 1970s—joined the even smaller group who achieved election the first time they were eligible for consideration, five years after retirement. I hadn't been to Cooperstown, and I figured I'd never pick a better time to make that trip that I had always wanted to make.

And I was right. A weekend of rain altered the ceremony but in no way dampened the emotional enthusiasm of an unbelievable entourage of those great Baltimore fans, who obviously cherished those championship days—and heroes. All of us were there for Jim, and in a way for ourselves because of the great times he represented. I think the outpouring surprised and genuinely pleased him.

Naturally, a lot of memories went through my mind during that three-day adventure in nostalgia. I thought of just how good he was. Had he not been disabled with back and shoulder problems for nearly two years, he would have easily won 300 games or more.

And I also remembered that some people in the Orioles organization thought Palmer imagined his various physical problems. I'll never forget hearing Harry Dalton argue very seriously in an organization meeting one time that Jim should be lined up with a psychiatrist.

Harry's idea came to mind in the spring of 1991 when Jim, at forty-five, actually went to spring training and tried for a comeback. Sure, it had to be eating at him that Roger Clemens had just signed a contract that paid him more money for pitching one year than Jim Palmer made in a whole Hall of Fame career. Jim always felt underpaid, even by the salaries of his day. The Orioles were not cheap, but Jim was one of those luckless guys. He'd work out a three-year contract at top dollar and feel good about it, then in the second year of that contract, the salary spiral would take off and he'd be sitting there holding a binding but outdated contract feeling cheated as hell.

He'd tell me, "Look at what they're paying me." And I'd say, "Jimmy, you signed a three-year contract. It isn't the club's fault." I didn't think he had the best of negotiating situations. He was the only player his agent represented. I just didn't feel the guy was in position to sense things such as salary spirals and I mentioned to Jim more than once that he should think about doing what most of our other guys had done: go with Ron Shapiro, in my opinion the best player agent in the business. Jim always responded to me, "The guy I've got is all right." I don't know whether he was stubborn or naive, but the guy who ultimately represented him—including the negotiations that got him his shot at forty-five—was Ron Shapiro.

I'd love to have seen Jim get one of those huge contracts. I'm not an old-timer who resents them, not when a Roger Clemens gets his $5 million or so. We're in an era when Michael Jackson can sign for $1 *billion*. Now, I'll concede without even knowing for sure that Clemens probably can't sing and dance as well as Jackson, but I'd say he would have a hell of a lot better chance of doing that than Jackson would of throwing or hitting a 90 mph fastball.

To me, it isn't the Clemens contracts that are threatening baseball, it's the ones just a little bit smaller going to journeyman pitchers like Clemens' teammate, Matt Young. That's what's scary.

Lure of the big money and all, Palmer's comeback try didn't work, of course, and I never thought it would. I had no doubts about Jim Palmer physically. Nobody takes better care of himself. But he was always a high-ball pitcher. Losing just a little bit off a high fastball—and being out of the game for more than five years almost guaranteed he had lost something—meant the ball no longer would rise for him, and the one that doesn't is the ball that good hitters jump out of their shoes to swing at.

And I never thought he could make the conversion to the bullpen. We made relievers of worn-out starters in the old days, but not today. Every year a whole new crop of them comes up, groomed for bullpen duty in the minor leagues. So, Jim brightened the spring for a lot of forty-year-olds by giving it an honest, inspiring try, and then saw enough himself to step out and stay retired—today's big money and all.

At the peak of his career, though, when Harry Dalton was dropping hints about head problems for Jim Palmer, I neither believed it nor liked it.

The idea obviously got as far as our owner, Edward Bennett Williams. He asked me once how many games I thought Palmer could win that season. I said I felt if he got 35 to 38 starts, he could win in the area of 18 to 20 games. His response was a question that indicated to me he had at least heard of Dalton's doubts and might be inclined to believe them himself:

"What if he complains about his arm hurting?"

I said, "Mr. Williams, if Jim Palmer says his arm is hurting, I have to believe him. It's his arm. He's the only one who knows."

And that's as straight as I can be with my boss. Only the pitcher knows. Not even a doctor feels the pain.

I suspect that I'd have been feeling some pain if that swollen knee that I had kept from our people had turned out to be career-ending, after I had given him our money. I'm not sure Jim ever appreciated the chance I took. I could have been fired.

But that little gamble had paid big dividends long before I sat in the audience at his Hall of Fame induction and just felt great—proud for him, for the Orioles, and you're damned right, proud for me. That day, that little act of trickery seemed like one of the wisest moves I ever made in my baseball life.

8

The Fine Art of Trading

The late Joe Reichler, whom I got to know and deeply respect from his days as an Associated Press baseball writer out of New York, really tickled me with what he had to say about the Frank Robinson trade in a book he published, *The Baseball Trade Register*:

"Trades, whether blockbusters or unnoticed transactions involving unknown ballplayers, can have a major impact on the pennant race, and can sometimes indicate or dictate the direction of a franchise. Without question, the great Baltimore Orioles clubs of the last two decades were turned from contenders to champions by the Frank Robinson trade of December 9, 1965."

Joe's book is an ambitious effort: a listing of every player sale or trade in every franchise's history—and a personal ranking of the five best and the five worst deals each team had made.

I have special memories of each of the four deals he ranked at the top of the Orioles' "Best" list—and one on the "Worst" list, too. I'll pass them along, because I think they illustrate what goes on behind the scenes when trades are made.

We'll take them in the order Reichler ranks them (right below the Robinson trade), which also happens to be the order in which they occurred.

2. *Mike Cuellar*, Enzo Hernandez and Elijah Johnson from the Houston Astros for *Curt Blefary* and John Mason, December 4, 1968.

This shows me something about Joe Reichler, because I don't think many people would rank this deal very highly. I'm with Joe. Mike Cuellar represents perhaps one of the most satisfying jobs I ever did in scouting, although I am pretty proud of the Frank Robinson situation because I had to fight.

I was always sort of intrigued by Cuellar, from the first time I saw him. He started out in the Cincinnati system, he was up briefly, and he was released to the Mexican League. The first I saw of him was after the Cardinals signed him. He was 5-5 for their world championship team in 1964. For them, he was just a mopup guy. The score's 7-1, we're getting beat, bring Cuellar in. I would sit there and watch, and I saw nothing but ground balls. I remembered, but I never gave it all that much thought, and he went back down to the minors the next year.

He was twenty-nine when Houston brought him up, and he went 12-10, 16-11 and 8-11. They started him some. I was starting to like him a little bit. It wasn't: "Oh, man, we've gotta get this guy." But the more I saw him the more I liked him.

In 1967, the year he went 16-11, he pitched two innings in the All-Star Game in Anaheim, and there was nothing but ground balls. Everybody likes him then. The next year, he has a losing season, he's thirty-one now, and his stock drops.

In the fall, most clubs bring their people in for four or five days to evaluate the entire organization and pinpoint the players in the other organizations that they like. Evaluating your own club well is the tough part. You tend to like your own players and give them the benefit of every doubt. This can lead you to the second division quicker than anything. That year, we had a problem and knew it. We came to the conclusion that we needed a left-handed starting pitcher.

I said, "I've got one. I just think Cuellar at Houston is a hell of a pitcher. I've seen him now for three years. I see nothing but ground balls. He throws strikes. He throws a good screwball now that he didn't use to have." When I'm sitting there, all I can think of is our infield: Brooks at third, Belanger at short, Johnson at second. This guy has got to be a hell of a pitcher for us because he throws so many ground balls.

So here's the way deals are put together. They said, "Jim, this guy had a losing year." I said, "Great. If he was 13-8, or 18-8, do you think he might be available? No way."

That's the time you've got to speak up, and be worth listening to. You can't tell your general manager, "Damn. This Clemens with the Red Sox is one hell of a pitcher." You've got no chance of getting Clemens—but some scouts do that. "Gee, I like that Sandberg; we ought to go after him." They ought to fire you when you talk like that. Anybody in the fourth grade knows Ryne Sandberg is a pretty damned good ballplayer—and untouchable.

But with Cuellar, we were talking about a guy I liked very much and he'd had a losing season. I was crazy about Mike. The more I saw him the more I thought was how good he would look in orange and black.

Houston was interested in Blefary—which makes him a figure in the trades Joe Reichler ranks first *and* second. Blefary had some pop in his bat, but what the Astros failed to take into consideration, I'm afraid, is that the Astrodome is the toughest park in baseball for hitters. You can just hit the hell out of the ball and somebody goes back and catches it. So we got together with Houston and made the deal.

Earl Weaver was a little cool about the deal. Frank Cashen, not knowing anything about Cuellar, said to Harry Dalton, "Don't you feel, though, that we still should continue to pursue a left-handed starter?" Frank didn't know me all that well at that time, although he had respect for me because of what he saw in the Robinson trade. Dalton said, "Jim says this is the guy who can do it."

But Weaver had managed against Cuellar in winter ball in

Puerto Rico and I think that's why he was unexcited. Down there, some pitchers don't go all out. Earl wasn't opposed to the trade, he was just lukewarm about it. Later on, when Cuellar won 23 ballgames for us, Earl said, "Well, hell, he looked good down there." He didn't mention that when the deal was being made.

Managers in general aren't the best people to have around when a deal is being made. Earl will do as an example.

At the 1974 winter meetings, we wanted to deal for some right-handed power and the obvious target was Lee May of Houston. Weaver loved power on his team, and I told him with May, "You can just start the year figuring he's going to hit .260, drive in 90 to 100 runs, and hit 25 to 30 home runs. He's a streak hitter. He'll be in a slump, then all of a sudden he'll get hot and carry the club."

Houston wanted a good-looking young second baseman in our farm system, Rob Andrews. We thought we had the deal all set, but Weaver was so eager to get Lee May's power on our club he told Preston Gomez, the Astros' manager, to push for the trade by demanding another player in addition to Andrews. We went in to close the deal, and Spec Richardson of Houston threw that curve at us. Eventually they got Enos Cabell, a good young athlete who could play anywhere in the infield or outfield and had some speed. We all heard about Weaver's role in the negotiating, and Frank Cashen was as angry as I ever saw him. We did go ahead and make the trade, but it cost us one more player than it should have.

I don't have the fondest memories of Earl, where trade talk is involved. In 1977, he tried to make me the goat of a story of incredibly bad intra-club communication. Earl knew we were close to making a deal with Montreal: primarily pitcher Rudy May for relief pitcher Don Stanhouse, who I thought had been one of the best relief pitchers in the National League the second half of that year.

We were talking with the Montreal people, but Weaver wasn't around. The place to find managers at the winter meetings is in the Topps (bubblegum) suite, where drinks are free.

Earl called up from there to where we were meeting and asked how things were going. I told him things could break any time and he probably should come on up. The drinks sounded better to Earl, who was still in the Topps suite when the trade was made, and announced. The press conference putting out the word was still going on when Weaver angrily walked in and started shouting at me for not telling him before the deal was made. He was dead wrong, and he's wrong when he discusses the incident in his autobiography. I did tell him he should come up, and I had people around who heard me say it. Earl was so angry he actually resigned. It never hit the papers before he had been talked out of it, but he didn't score any points with our ownership that day for the way he made an ass of himself and embarrassed me and our whole organization.

But I could take a little embarrassment over a Stanhouse trade and still be way ahead for the satisfaction I felt—at the time of the deal and forever after—over the trade that got us Mike Cuellar. Maybe more than in any other trade I was involved in, I felt like I did the thing that a good scout is supposed to do: project in your mind what you think this guy can be for you. And secondly, I could have turned into a pussycat and been very defensive because he had a losing record. I could have said, "If he has the same record for us, I could lose my job." That never occurred to me; it never bothered me. I always have had the courage of my convictions. I felt real good about Cuellar, and the man never let me down.

3. *Mike Torrez* and *Ken Singleton* from the Montreal Expos for *Dave McNally, Rich Coggins* and Bill Kirkpatrick, December 4, 1974.

We're at the winter meetings, talking with Montreal, and they like McNally and Coggins. I liked Singleton and Torrez. Torrez had had a 15-8 year for them, and Singleton could hit blindfolded—a hell of a hitter. Singleton is one of the greatest guys ever to put a uniform on but also one of the best hitters, and those two things don't always go together.

Singleton was a switch-hitter, with maybe as good a conception of the strike zone as anybody we ever had. Because of that, one whole year Weaver batted him leadoff, as slow as Singleton was. Weaver wasn't worried about the speed. He wanted to get him on base, so he could lay back and wait for that three-run homer. That image he had of loving three-run homers was no myth.

Gene Mauch was the Montreal manager at the time of the trade. Because Singleton was a big guy who couldn't run and who wasn't a real good defensive player, he wasn't Mauch's type of player. I could see what they liked in Coggins: an outfielder, left-handed, great speed, a pretty good hitter. A glandular problem, and not the best of attitudes, kept him from being what he might have been, but he was a good-looking prospect.

The Expos were very interested in McNally. Obviously, McNally was special to all of us, especially me, but we were to the point where we would make McNally expendable. Cashen and I are in their suite, with Mauch, John McHale and Jim Fanning there for them. Fanning said, "This sounds fine to us, but I think we have to have another ballplayer in the deal from you."

I can understand his thinking. They're fairly new in Montreal. They want to show the press where they got three for two. Frank said, "I just don't think we can do that," which was a good response. I turned to Mauch and said, "Gene, you know that John Montague who you got from us—what do you think of him?" He said, "At times, he's looked great." Montague—great? That's overuse of the word. God. Great belongs with Sandy Koufax or Jim Palmer, but I didn't mind hearing him say it. I said, "Well, we've got a pitcher at Rochester named Bill Kirkpatrick whose stuff is as good as Montague's. They're pretty close to being alike. Would you be interested if we put him in the deal?" Fanning said, "Let me call our manager in the International League."

He made the call right there, and the manager said, "Yeah, Kirkpatrick has a chance." Fanning said, "You've got a deal."

That's the way deals are made. It always pays to have some Bill Kirkpatricks around.

But I never was in on another deal with the Expos. They never forgave me for that one—particularly after McNally, only thirty-two at the time, went 3-6 with Montreal and retired before the year was over, because he didn't want to take the Expos' money when he wasn't getting batters out. Maybe to Montreal that was just one last act in a bad trade, but to me it was one more example of the pure class of Dave McNally.

4. *Scott McGregor, Tippy Martinez, Rick Dempsey, Rudy May* and Dave Pagan from the New York Yankees for *Doyle Alexander, Ken Holtzman, Grant Jackson, Elrod Hendricks* and Jimmy Freeman, June 15, 1976.

I might have wanted to argue a little bit with Joe on this one. I would have ranked it a little higher, for what it did for our club. The players we obtained were a big part of our team for the rest of the 1970s and into the 1980s.

This trade is an illustration of the difference between being in a position where you want to win right now, or where you know you're not ready to win yet and you're trying to help yourself for the future. They're both legitimate positions, and that's why trades can be good for both teams, even though they may look a little one-sided for one in the first year or two and one-sided the other way long-term. That's what this deal was all about. We were thinking about the future and the Yankees needed immediate help.

You'll notice that unlike those other trades, which were made at the winter meetings, this one came in mid-season. Gabe Paul ran the Yankees at the time. They were just sure they could win the division and the pennant if they had a veteran left-hander on their staff, and we had Holtzman. Hank Peters set up an appointment with Gabe in Chicago. I forget whether we went up to his suite or he came to ours, but I do know he was pretty well loaded. We're talking and talking and kicking names back and forth because they really wanted Holtzman. But to every name we mentioned, Gabe would say, ''No, no, I can't do that.''

We finally got him to pretty much agree on a couple of the names and I said, ''Well, what about Ron Guidry?'' He said,

''We'd be interested in talking about him, too.'' Then he backed off. He said, ''Guys, look, I've had a few drinks tonight. Why don't we talk in the morning?'' Well, you can't say no to something like that.

So we sat down the next morning, went through the whole deal again, and he said no to everybody we mentioned. Quite a few of the guys weren't even in the big leagues yet—they were still down at Syracuse, for Christ's sake, including McGregor—but he kept saying, ''Oh, we can't do that.''

Hank hadn't really been involved in a deal of this magnitude before. He kept saying, ''Wait a minute, Jim and I will go in the next room and talk.'' We did that a couple of times and finally I said, ''Hank, dammit, let's just stay right with our position and to hell with it. If he wants Holtzman, he's gonna have to pay for Holtzman.''

The reason we wanted a lot of the Yankee farm players in the deal was because Clyde Kluttz had come to us from New York. He was their farm director, so he knew all the kids in their farm system. That was a big help to us.

Let me digress for just a minute here to say that if I were an owner, this is an area that would raise a red flag to me every time: a prospective trade with a club that has just brought in somebody who had been involved with player development for you. One of the great steals of modern time came in 1982 when Dallas Green had just gone from Philadelphia to the Cubs, and he let the Phils talk him out of a pretty good shortstop of the day, Ivan DeJesus, even up for shortstop Larry Bowa...with just a little sweetener, a 20th-round draft choice named Ryne Sandberg. Sandberg at the time had one single in the major leagues, but Green knew he had been a 20th-rounder because he was an outstanding quarterback prospect coming out of high school who had signed with Washington State. Everyone else laid off him, but the Phillies took a chance late and landed him, but only Green in that Phils organization apparently knew what a jewel they had. What our Yankee trade in 1976 said and that Cub-Phils trade in 1982 underlined was: Never, never deal with a transplanted insider—but if the guy's on your side and you find someone who will, get to the table as fast you can.

We went back in and Gabe continued to back off: "We can't part with him...the press will kill me if we part with him."

After about an hour or so of that crap, I said, "Gabe, I want to tell you something. You might not get Holtzman. You might not win the division and the pennant. But you'll be able to tell the press, 'We didn't win the division, fellas. We didn't win the pennant. But by God we kept those kids in Syracuse.'

"Is that what you want? Are you going to let the press dictate whether you win the division or not? You're getting the veteran left-hander you want, the guy you asked for—and you're telling us we can't have anybody.'"

I think that got to him. I don't think anybody had ever talked to him like that. Finally we agreed on the deal the way it was made. But I'll tell you what: We might have been close to getting Guidry, had Gabe not said, "Fellas, I've had a few drinks. Let's carry this on tomorrow."

It turned out to be a hell of a deal for us, and not a bad one for them. They won the pennant in 1976 with Holtzman. They were just that close to being able to get the job done. Yeah, they were losing something, but we weren't tapping anything of immediate help to them. Dempsey was behind Thurman Munson, for example, and Tippy Martinez was behind Sparky Lyle—way behind. Dempsey came over and did a hell of a job for us, for years. Tippy Martinez became our No. 1 left-handed reliever, and one of the best. One of the ironies of that trade was that for years after that every time we went into Yankee Stadium, with its short right-field fence, Earl always had two of the guys in that deal, McGregor and Martinez, plus Mike Flanagan rested and ready to combat those Yankee left-handed hitters.

The point of the trade was that we were tapping some futures, and you're never too sure about them. It worked out nicely for both of us.

Then there were the deals that didn't work out so well.

Joe Reichler lists our club's all-time worst trade as Vic Wertz to the Cleveland Indians for Bob Chakales in 1954. That one would have looked a hell of a lot worse if Wertz had hit that World Series drive one foot farther and gotten it over Willie Mays, but I didn't have anything to do with that deal.

From there Reichler's "worst" list goes:

2. *Dave Johnson, Pat Dobson,* Roric Harrison and Johnny Oates to the Atlanta Braves for *Earl Williams* and Taylor Duncan, December 30, 1972.

I definitely was in on that one. I'll admit it. I thought it was an outstanding deal for us.

I blame Henry Aaron for why it wasn't. But I'll get to that.

Let's reconstruct the situation. We've had our big years with the Robinsons and that's over. In 1972, we slip to third in our division, and we're getting old.

You know how much I loved Dave Johnson. But Dave's turning thirty now, he had hit only .221 for us that year and missed a lot of games, and we've got an awfully good young second baseman named Bobby Grich who is ready to play. We had sent both Grich and Don Baylor back to Rochester that year when they could have played in the big leagues for a lot of ballclubs. Hell, they were ready to play for us, but we thought we were so good we didn't need them and we wanted them to play, so we sent them out. I knew it was a tough thing, but they both were nice about it: "We'll go back another year and then when we come up again we'll be here to stay." That's the kind of thing we had going on the Orioles then, and sometimes you don't take into account how much that kind of attitude means.

We did, after this trade.

But anyway, Grich was ready and it made Johnson expendable. I had spoken to the Atlanta general manager, Eddie Robinson, a lot. He was going to make Williams available, and he had been Rookie of the Year just a year earlier when he hit 33 home runs. I had seen Williams in the National League, and Walter Youse, our Eastern scouting supervisor, had seen him, too. We discussed Williams, and I said, "Jesus, you don't get that kind of production out of a catcher very often (61 homers his first two years up, and 87 RBI each year). He can help our ballclub."

When we made the deal, Weaver gave the writers a rather liberal interpretation of what I had said: "Russo says he might hit 40 home runs for me and we're a cinch to win the pennant and the World Series with Earl Williams." I *never* made a statement like that. I'm not *that* stupid. But I did say he would hit some home runs for us, maybe close to 30, and he'd drive in some runs for us.

I wasn't wrong about that, but where I was wrong was in not having checked more thoroughly into Williams as a person. His makeup was just terrible. This guy really, really gave us a hard time.

The very first spring training, Williams leaves the field while we're still working out and goes into the clubhouse. In the Orioles' spring training camp, nobody leaves the field and goes into the clubhouse. No way. I don't give a damn if you're Mickey Mantle, you don't leave the field in the Baltimore Orioles' spring training camp and go to the clubhouse. Weaver sees that, gets hold of Earl Williams, and the two of them just go around and around and around.

Then Weaver gets me: "So this is the son of a bitch that you told me would lead us to the World Series and would hit 40 home runs." I said, "Now, goddammit, don't start that shit. I didn't say he'd hit 40 home runs. Yeah, his makeup disappoints me. But I'm going to tell you something else. Maybe it's not his fault, and I'm not trying to defend myself. On the Atlanta ballclub right now—during the season or spring training, it doesn't make any difference—everybody does what they want to do. And the reason is because No. 44 does anything he wants to do. If they see him go into the clubhouse they think, 'Well, hell, I can go into the clubhouse, too.'" No. 44, of course, was their superstar, Henry Aaron.

Weaver knows I'm right, but he goes on, "What do you think my other players are saying when they see him do that?" Now I'm starting to get heated up, and I said, "Earl, I can't go out here and get you twenty-five angels. You're getting paid to handle some of these guys.''

I was upset, because Earl would do that. Whenever a ball-player would give him a little bit of a rough time, he'd run to me right away and say, ''Reggie [Jackson] is testing me. He's start-ing to come into the clubhouse five minutes late one day and maybe ten minutes later another day.'' Hey, at that time we were paying him $200,000 to $300,000 a year to manage the damned ballclub, and he's complaining to me when ballplayers might be testing him, just to see what he was going to do about it. When you're making that kind of money, you're supposed to handle situations like that.

The season started, and things didn't get any better. Earl Williams just made an ass out of himself, and his wife was worse. There's a television station in Baltimore that would have the wives on, and people would call in. They had Williams' wife on one day, and she said, ''We can't wait till we get out of this damned town.'' God almighty.

And Williams himself is giving everybody a hard time. I sat down and talked to him one time: ''Earl, let me tell you some-thing. This is not Atlanta. This is the Baltimore Orioles. You just came from a horseshit ballclub and a horseshit organization, and you could get away with anything you wanted to do. I'm not pin-ning all the blame on you, because you didn't have a very good example when it came to your so-called leader. He could do any-thing he wanted to do so I'm pretty sure the rest of you thought that if he could get away with it, you could get away with it.'' He said, ''Yeah, that's the way it was.''

I said, ''That's not the way we do it here. This is the Ori-oles. We have a lot of pride—probably more pride than any other organization in baseball, including the Yankees. Some of the things you've done we just don't do in this organization. Your walking off the field to go into the clubhouse because it's a little cooler in there—Orioles don't do that, and you're not going to do it.''

He just couldn't understand those things. I said, ''One of these days you'll learn that what we're trying to tell you is because we're trying to help you. It all fits into trying to make you a better ballplayer." He just never got it, and it disappointed me. An example: more than once, in our ballpark, he got hold of a ball pretty well and drove it deep but someone caught it near the fence—a home run in Atlanta. Sure, it would exasperate Williams. It bothers any good hitter to come close to a home run and miss. But Williams would come all the way back to the dugout and on the top step, just as he was about to disappear from view, he'd scream "Fuck!" The closest seats to the dugout belonged to the nicest guy in the world, Jerry Hoffberger, who would have his wife and a party of friends there, and be very embarrassed. I told Williams: "For Christ's sake, at least wait till you're *in* the dugout before you shout stuff like that." He never understood. He threw away much of a truly promising career and wound up playing in the Mexican League, reduced to running ads in *The Sporting News* offering his services to any club that was interested. When I saw one of those, the thought that went through my mind was a little cynical: "I wonder how his wife likes those towns in Mexico."

But I will say one more thing. With Earl Williams in 1973, we won our division, and he certainly contributed. He drove in 83 runs and had 22 home runs. Weaver gave me all that hell, but in calmer moments he would say, "We might not have won the division without him." That's good production out of a catcher, and I'll say this for Earl Williams: he knew how to read those figures. He could point out where in certain years he was more productive than Johnny Bench was per at bat or something.

All I know was I sure would have preferred to have had Johnny Bench.

And that's another story. It makes me sick to this day to think how easily we could have had Johnny Bench. We *should* have had Johnny Bench. The Cincinnati Reds didn't find Johnny Bench in Binger, Oklahoma, and I know that for the most painful of reasons. I saw him, and I'm the one who told Cincinnati about him.

It was all above board, and it wasn't a mistake. It was 1965, the first year baseball had a free agent draft, and our two clubs had decided to exchange scouting information. I was supposed to give them what I had. It doesn't sound too smart now, and I wasn't too excited with it then, but that's the way it was.

Richard Horton. That's the guy who cost me Johnny Bench.

Jim McLaughlin had made the switch from Baltimore to Cincinnati by then, and Walter Shannon was running our scouting department. McLaughlin and Shannon got together and decided to exchange information. Cincinnati was strong in some parts of the country where we weren't, and we were strong in some areas where Cincinnati wasn't. Now, there is a Central Scouting Bureau available to all clubs, so that kind of arrangement is unnecessary.

Too bad it wasn't then, because that year I discovered a gem when I went in to see a kid at Tulsa. Byron Humphrey, who was covering Oklahoma for us, said, "There's a kid in a real little town south of Oklahoma City that I've seen just one time but I kind of like him. He doesn't play many games, but I know other guys are talking about him, too. He's pretty good." They played Legion ball at Binger when their very short high school season—about eight games—was over. He was in Legion play when I went in and took a look at him. He caught and, of course, I was very impressed. I felt *real* good about him. Just a one-game look, but you feel good or you don't. I liked him as a catcher, and I liked the way he swung the bat.

Cincinnati had a good scout in that area, Ray Baker, but that year he was sick. He had played in the Brownie organization and his brother, Floyd, was an infielder in the big leagues—a great glove man, "Baker the Blotter," White Sox radio announcer Bob Elson used to call him when he was playing for them. But, anyway, shortly after I was in there, Ray Baker died.

So McLaughlin called me one day, since we were exchanging information, and he said, "Who have you seen that you like?" I said, "Do you have anything on a kid named John Bench in Binger, Oklahoma?" He said, "Just a second." He came back on the phone and said, ''I've got nothing on him.'' I said, ''You'd better send someone in there to look at him.'' We hung up.

Jim was good at his job. He not only sent in the closest scout he had, Tony Robello, who was living in Fort Worth at the time, he also sent in Bob Thurman, who had been a good major league hitter with the Reds and was one of Jim's top people. Naturally, they loved the guy.

Now it's time for the draft. We started getting things in order—No. 1, 2, 3, 4, all the way down the line. I said, ''I like Bench very much. He's as good-looking a player as I've seen this spring. If we put him No. 1, it wouldn't upset me. There might be some pretty good-looking ballplayers in the country—I haven't seen them all—but this guy is good enough to be my first choice.''

Harry Dalton, of all guys, said, ''No, we're going to take a catcher from the East that I saw myself. A guy by the name of Horton, from Dartmouth.'' And he reiterated, ''I saw him myself.'' Here's a guy who never scouted saying he saw this guy himself so he's going to be the first player we take. It killed me.

Then Jimmy McLaughlin was so smart. I know he said to himself, ''We like Bernie Carbo in Michigan. Everybody knows about him. Bench is from this little town—he hasn't had that much exposure among the big league scouts. He just might still be there in the second round.'' They took Carbo in the first round and got Bench, too, because we—picking one spot ahead of them—wasted our picks on a pitcher named Scott McDonald and our find from Dartmouth. I was sick—for about fifteen years.

We made one other mistake that fits right in with that one.

I always liked to keep as close a working relationship as I could with the top people on every club, in both leagues. I worked at it. Say if I was working the National League, maybe my schedule would keep me in the same city for two series. Sometime in there, I would go up to the club office, sit down with the general manager and say, ''What are you guys going to be looking for? Here's what we may have available." When I did that with the Cubs, they let me know they were interested in Mike Epstein, who was a hot young prospect in our farm system.

And at the winter meetings, they followed up on that by telling me how interested they were. They said they *might* be willing to make Billy Williams available.

I couldn't believe it. I thought to myself, "Oh, my God. First Frank Robinson, and now this guy? Billy Williams in *our* lineup, with Frank and Brooks and Boog?"

I went back and told our people. Poor Hank Bauer couldn't contain himself. I've said Hank wasn't overly eager to give up Milt Pappas for Frank Robinson, but Hank didn't have any reservations at all about Billy Williams. He had a big smile on his face he was so happy, and he said, "My God, where would I hit him?" My answer was "Anywhere. If he was mine, I'd hit him third. But anywhere." Hank and I were like little kids, almost giddy at this totally unexpected possibility. And Hank would tell you today that he already had doodled around with a lineup, with Williams batting third.

Pretty soon Leo Durocher, who was managing the Cubs, is in the room, with their general manager, John Holland. We're talking, and we're all happy because it sounds like we're going to be able to make the deal.

Let me say one thing right here: A lot of people criticized Durocher, but seeing him close-up in this situation, I thought he was fantastic—perfectly honest and above board. He told us he wanted Epstein because they needed a left-handed hitter with power and a first baseman who could play the position well. Yes, they did have Ernie Banks there, but he was thirty-six and starting to slow down. To this day, I don't know what the Cubs had in mind for him if they got Epstein. I can't imagine the Cubs trading Ernie Banks, or benching Ernie Banks. I'm sure Leo had it planned out, but I never got a chance to ask him about it before he died in 1991.

But *we* didn't make the deal. We dropped it.

Not right away. When Durocher and Holland left—it must

have been three or four in the morning—they thought they had a trade, I'm sure. Frank Cashen was the one who said after they closed the door behind them: "Wait a minute. Let's not get in a hurry about moving Epstein. I've got 400 Jewish box seat holders who come to our ballpark. It would upset our budget if we piss them off and they don't come out to the ballpark." Dalton said, "I don't think we can move Epstein. As far as I'm concerned, he's going to be a superstar."

I got a little pissed off then, and Hank Bauer was right with me. I said, "If we get Billy Williams, the Jewish people will be just like everybody else, knocking the gates down to get in the ballpark and see this club play." But Frank and Harry had it in their minds that Mike Epstein was going to be the next great Jewish player. Epstein had just been named Minor League Player of the Year—he was twenty-three, and he had 29 homers and 102 RBI at our Triple-A team, Rochester. He was going to be our link to the Jewish community in the whole Baltimore area.

Weird as it sounds, I don't hold it against Frank Cashen for his reasoning. Demographics is a new word but an old idea. Who knows? The Jewish population in Skokie might have entered into the Cubs' thinking, too. But, damn! We weren't talking about Hank Greenberg here. Epstein just simply wasn't as good a ball-player as the Orioles—and the Cubs, obviously—thought he was. The thing that upset the hell out of me was I thought Frank and Harry should have understood that I knew more than they did about Billy Williams' ability to help the Orioles because I saw a hell of a lot more of him.

So we said no. To Billy Williams.

And barely a month into the 1967 season, after Epstein had been in exactly six games for us with all of eleven times at bat, we shipped him to the Senators for a pitcher named Pete Richert.

All Billy Williams did was shake off a couple of .270 years, get that beautiful swing of his grooved and hit his way into the Hall of Fame.

I'll get reckless here. I think he would have helped us more than Pete Richert, or Mike Epstein...or a thousand Pete Richerts and Mike Epsteins.

Dynasty is not a word I like to throw around, but we were pretty good in the 1970s anyway. Imagine us with Johnny Bench catching and Billy Williams in left.

And in both cases, we were the reason it didn't happen.

9

Payoff Time

All the spadework, all the scouting and all the trading don't mean a damned thing if there aren't some championships to show for it.

So here we are. Dodger Stadium. World Series 1966.

What a feeling. That's a quarter-century ago now and I still feel it. Of the hundreds of thousands of pitches I watched and hits I charted and plays I saw, nothing matches the way I felt watching those back-to-back, Robinson-and-Robinson home runs sail into the stands in the top of the first in Game 1.

In baseball, you do learn to come back to earth in a hurry, no matter how high you get. If you don't, the game has a way of burying you under that earth. Fast.

I thought of that as I sat down after cheering Brooks Robinson all the way around the bases. We had a 3-0 lead, and that was nice, but they hadn't even batted yet. I was still scared, and so was the man in the seat beside me: Frank Lane, "Trader" Lane in his days as general manager for the Go-Go White Sox in the Paul Richards days and later with Cleveland, where he had the brass to trade home-run champion Rocky Colavito for batting-average champion Harvey Kuenn, and manager Joe Gordon for manager Jimmy Dykes. Those are stunts that no other general manager has dared to try since (maybe in part because it all didn't work out too well: in a two-year period after the Colavito trade, the Indians went from second to fifth and attendance dropped by more than half—which meant good-bye, Trader Lane).

Frank was out of a job when Lee MacPhail hired him into our organization as a sort of adviser. He and I were sitting together in the Orioles' box, way out in the right-field stands. The location of the box was a reminder that we were new at this World Series business. It's standard in baseball now to put the visiting team's official party in a box near the team's dugout, usually right next to it. It became standard because we raised some hell, behind the scenes and with the right people, over our treatment at Los Angeles in 1966. It didn't change anything—to this day the Dodgers refuse to let scouts sit behind the plate, pompously claiming that they can't because the seats are so valuable they have to make them available to season ticket buyers. Everybody else in baseball finds a way to preserve that one key section. In the pre-Marge Schott days, the Reds got so mad about it they offered to buy seats so their scouts could do their job right—and were damned well going to charge the Dodgers when they came to Riverfront. Ultimately, the seats did get a little better, but that glorious day in October 1966, the new kids on the World Series block from Baltimore watched from right field, which made what we wound up seeing in that Series even a little bit sweeter.

In the opening game, Dave McNally was pitching for us—my guy McNally, my man from Montana pitching against the organization that was so mad when we got him and they didn't.

The first man up was Maury Wills, and he walked him.

"JEE-zus, Dave," I'm screaming, and Lane is louder. Lines in the scouting report I had prepared exploded in my mind and I wondered how McNally had missed them:

"Don't fool around with him. Give him good hard stuff and keep him off the bases...

"Keep him off base if at all possible. A great part of their offense revolves around Wills getting on base..."

Now, those lines, of course, didn't stamp me as one of the all-time great sleuths. This wasn't the Wills who had stolen 104 bases in 1962. In fact, he was a little gimpy in one knee coming into the Series, and I'll give you an insight to just how ruthless a baseball opponent can get when there's a World Series championship on the line. This is straight from that scouting report:

"Even with his bad knee, he still gives the pitcher trouble when on base and will be a threat to steal...Make him use his bad leg as often as possible. By this we mean the pitcher throwing to first base...often. Also, the catcher throwing to first. Or second. Let's aggravate the knee as much as possible." Drysdale didn't have a corner on meanness.

But here is McNally, with a 3-0 lead, *giving* Wills first base. What that told me was McNally, as good a competitor as we had, was pitching the way I felt—nervous as hell. Why not? It was his first World Series, too. The people from Billings had sent one of those long telegrams with about a thousand names. He got that at the hotel in Los Angeles. He's just a kid, twenty-three years old. You can imagine how he felt—the way we all did, just happy as hell that we were even there.

He was throwing hard; he had great stuff. He couldn't get it over the plate. Even from right field I could see his release point was high, so he was throwing the ball high. There was no doubt in my mind he had jitters.

He got out of that all right, and we scored again in the second, so now we were up 4-0.

Then Jim Lefebvre homered, Wes Parker doubled, Junior Gilliam walked, and I said, "Frank, I can't stand this any more. Let's walk around." We got up and just paced, back and forth.

Dave survived, on a line drive pulled down in right-center and a blast by Dick Stuart, pinch-hitting for Drysdale, that Frank Robinson caught in front of the right-centerfield wall, a few feet from wiping out our lead.

With one out in the third, McNally walked three men in a

row, and that was all Hank Bauer could take. He called in Moe Drabowsky.

Moe once had been considered a very good prospect—Dick Drott and Drabowsky were rookies together with the Cubs in 1957, and both of them threw the hell out of the ball: 170 strike-outs each, 28 wins, 15 by Drott, who at twenty was a year younger than Moe but destined to be out of baseball long before thirty.

Moe stayed in baseball, but barely. His link with fame was serving up Stan Musial's 3,000th hit. He had some arm problems and bounced around with four clubs, going 48-81 and slipping back to the minors. That's where he was when we took a chance on him in the December 1965 winter draft. Here he was, the first man we turned to for rescue. In the World Series.

When the Series was over, Bill Leggett of *Sports Illustrated* made my scouting report a focus point for his World Series account. "Russo noted that Gaylord Perry of the Giants had given them trouble by using fastballs and a hard slider [plus an occasional spitter]. Russo also saw that Larry Dierker, a hard-throwing young pitcher for the Astros, gave the Dodgers trouble with fastballs." The term kept coming up on almost every hitter they had except Tommy Davis: "Hard stuff." That winter, I went to the New York writers' dinner, where Wes Parker said, "Where the hell did you come up with this 'hard stuff' business?" I said, "Hell, I stayed with you guys for twenty-two games. You ought to be able to learn something." He said, "You nailed it right on the head. We actually hit the curve ball better all year than we did the good fastball."

Before we left for Los Angeles, we spent two hours with the players going over that report—too long, really, but this was the first time and I didn't want to leave anything out. I was a little nervous, standing up there and going through it with them. You've got guys like Frank Robinson looking at you, and you're saying, "This guy's best pitch is...this is what he's going to throw." And Frank's seen the guy more than I have.

But Frank was great. When he had something to contribute, he did, and when a guy like that is so involved, I'll guarantee you the other players were probably thinking, "We'd better listen to everything." We even gave them each a copy of the report to read on the plane going out. We didn't do that in subsequent World Series—but, come to think of it, maybe we should have. We never swept anybody after that, either.

I do remember Frank looked at me just a little bit funny when we got to the fielding segment and I said about Junior Gilliam at third, "You can test him, as far as laying one down." Frank remembered a Gilliam who was impossible to bunt on, as quick as anyone who ever played that spot, but from that look, I don't think Frank realized that Junior, about to turn thirty-eight, finally was on his way down.

They were a tough ballclub to scout. Everybody in the infield was a switch-hitter, and there's never been a switch-hitter who hit exactly the same way left-handed and right-handed. What it worked out to was one guy, two different swing patterns, two different scouting reports. It gave the catcher more things to remember. You had to pitch them one way when they hit right-handed and another way when they turned around.

But we didn't vary it a whole lot. In the main, I told the pitchers to stick with the hard stuff either way.

So, in the fourth inning of that opener, we're up 4-1, the bases are loaded, Wes Parker is up, and here comes Drabowsky. I can't swear that Moe didn't sleep through our scouting meeting. I can't be sure he read one line of the sixteen-page report. I can't, because Moe's approach would have been the same if he had or hadn't. If I wanted hard stuff, I couldn't have gone to a better source than Moe Drabowsky. That was Moe's game.

He blew Parker away on strikes, then wobbled a little and walked Gilliam to force in a run. Now, Frank Lane is getting emotional. He's yelling at Drabowsky, "Throw the damned ball over the plate." OK, so he had walked in a run, but he wasn't the first guy ever worked for a walk by Junior Gilliam. I said, "Frank, all he's doing is throwing the hell out of the ball."

He kept it up. He went the rest of the way, shut out the Dodgers on one single, and struck out 11, still the World Series record for a relief pitcher.

God bless Moe Drabowsky. Hank Bauer had made a really good move that day. He sent all of his pitchers to the bullpen at the start of the game except the two young kids who were going to start the next two games, Jim Palmer and Wally Bunker. They sat right there in the dugout and watched Drabowsky bust the ball past the Dodgers all day long and their faith in the scouting report had to grow with every strike, and strikeout. Hard stuff. The message got across.

We won, 5-2, and it's hard to describe how pleasant that evening was. I really felt good. Winning that first game just took a whole big load off our shoulders. It just felt so good, having Frank Robinson on your side. He had been in these big things before. The rest of us hadn't.

Betty and I went with Jim Palmer's parents for a drink at one of those restaurants on the top story of the hotel, looking out over the city and all those lights. What a feeling.

Before we went up, we all talked with Jim in the hotel lobby. Here's a guy twenty years old who's going to be starting in the World Series the next day, against Sandy Koufax.

I asked him, "How do you feel about pitching against Koufax tomorrow?"

He said, "I can't wait."

God, that sounded great to me. It wasn't cockiness, it was confidence, but there's nothing wrong with a pitcher being a little cocky, too. I want a guy thinking he can go out there and win. That little exchange flashed through my mind when I sat in the crowd at Cooperstown in August 1990 and watched James Alvin Palmer's induction into the Hall of Fame. Koufax beat him there, but he didn't beat him in Dodger Stadium. In fact, the last game Hall of Fame-bound Sandy Koufax pitched was a 6-0 loss to up-and-coming Hall of Famer Jim Palmer.

But. . . Sandy Koufax.

I'll never forget the feeling I had standing up in front of our club and talking to them about how they could beat Sandy Koufax. I thought, "What in the hell can *I* tell them? The guys who have been in the National League know about this guy. Hell, everybody does."

I wound up talking longer about Koufax than any of their other players. Those whole three weeks, I kept seeing that rising fastball. A lot of them left his hand as a strike, but he threw so hard his ball would rise, so when it came across the plate it was actually a ball. He was getting a lot of help from the hitters. I saw that game after game, and I told our guys, ''I know it's hard to lay off of, because the guy is throwing so damn hard, but this is a lack of discipline. You have to discipline yourself when you walk up there and face a fastball like that, if it's rising, you take it.''

I almost pleaded with them: ''You have to concentrate and discipline yourself not to help him out, because he doesn't need any help.''

And I thought I had noticed something else. When he wasn't getting the curve ball over—and he had a hell of a curve, nasty—it looked to me like he abandoned it in a hurry. ''Not for the whole game, but for right now,'' I told our guys. ''He may come back with it an inning later, but in the games I saw if he wasn't getting it over for a strike, he'd quit throwing it and go with the fastball.''

But the primary thing that I tried to stress against Koufax was: You have to discipline yourself and try to swing at the ball in the strike zone.

They listened. He struck out just two hitters.

Now, the way the game started may not have made other things in my report look so good to our guys.

Luis Aparicio led off with an infield hit to deep short.

Remember the line in the scouting report about Koufax's pickoff move?

''Below-average move to first. Because of big windup, would try to steal on him. Doesn't throw often to first base; would steal on first movement and go regardless of the count.''

Aparicio, our best baserunner, broke for second on Koufax's first movement—and got picked off, Koufax to Wes Parker to Maury Wills, covering second.

OK, so he listened, gambled and got caught.

The point was: They did listen.

In fairness to Koufax, a 0-0 game broke open in the fifth when Willie Davis—whom the scouting report called ''a good outfielder, but not great because he doesn't always get a good jump on the ball''—lost two balls in the sun for errors and drew a third with a wild throw, a nightmare inning in the glare of the World Series for a really wonderful athlete. The three runs that inning went down as unearned, but not unnoticed or unappreciated. Jim Palmer made them look like thirty with an overpowering four-hit shutout that was his first huge step toward Cooperstown.

After the game, we flew back to Baltimore on the American League charter. Nestor Chylak was on board. He had worked that second game behind the plate. I thought he was the best umpire in the American League then, and for a number of years, just as Al Barlick was in the National League, and I told him, ''You did a hell of a job today.''

He said, ''I knew he was nervous [referring to Palmer], and I sure as hell was nervous. I made up my mind I was going to call the best game I ever called.''

Back in Baltimore, down 0-2, I think even the Dodgers knew every edge, even the psychological ones, had switched to the Orioles. I know our guys surely felt that way when 10,000 people were there at the airport to greet them. They call St. Louis a great baseball town, and it is—outstanding. But I don't know of too many times when 5,000 to 10,000 people have met the Cardinals at the airport, like they always did when we were in the World Series.

The Dodgers knew their one remaining chance was to win Game 3 with Claude Osteen and come back with Drysdale and Koufax. Osteen pitched beautifully, but made one mistake, a home-run ball that Paul Blair hit the hell out of—430 feet to left field. That was all Wally Bunker needed. Wally had had shoulder problems for a couple of years—he could pitch, but it hurt like hell. But what a heart he had. He was in pain with almost every pitch in that third game, but he made that Blair run stand up with a six-hit shutout. It was a gutty exhibition.

Now it was Dave McNally's turn again, and that was good.

It was kind of hard to imagine that Davey would have two bad games in a row. I always felt good when McNally was pitching.

And that day McNally—the real McNally, not the one who couldn't quite get settled down in the opener—gave us one more 1-0 win.

The Orioles ended that Series with three shutouts in a row, and a World Series record of thirty-three consecutive scoreless innings. The Dodgers in that Series hit .142.

We didn't exactly crush the ball, either. My scouting report helped us pound those Dodger pitchers at a .200 clip.

But it was good enough, because of Moe Drabowsky, Jim Palmer, Wally Bunker, Dave McNally, and a few other guys— one of them named Frank Robinson.

The one run in that fourth game, the run that made us world champions, came on another home run off Drysdale by Frank Robinson.

The one that got us started and the one that took us across the finish line both illustrated the No. 1 point I have always made when Frank Robinson's name came up. This guy didn't hit his home runs when the score was 11-2 or 8-0. This guy was just the best clutch hitter I ever saw.

10

Some Glory and Some Grief

Life was not all championships for the Orioles, even after we reached the top. But the living was pretty good. There's a line by Shakespeare that says, "They laugh that win." We did a lot of laughing for a lot of years.

We had a major falloff in 1967, mainly because Frank Robinson got hurt in midyear and missed about thirty games and partly because we were learning to live with success. The season wasn't very far along before Harry Dalton was upset with the way we were playing and sent me in to look at the club. After eight games, I concluded that the biggest thing wrong with us had nothing to do with talent. Our guys were just not in good condition—fat cats, after one year at the top. That's motivation, and that's part of the manager's job. When things weren't going a whole lot better halfway through the 1968 season, the club made the managerial switch from Hank Bauer to Earl Weaver.

That was the last major key. For the next fifteen years, we played just under .600 baseball, and that's a pretty difficult rate to accomplish for even just one year. It takes a 98-win season to reach .600, and if that doesn't win a championship, it will come damned close—any year.

No other club in either league was within seventy games of us over that stretch, which happened to be the first fifteen years of divisional play. Over much of that period, the American League East was considered the strongest in baseball, and we were the main reason—with some help from our original targets, the Yankees.

We got back to the World Series in 1969 with the best team in baseball. We didn't win the Series—didn't even come close, really. We lost in five games to the team they called the Miracle Mets. I'm not sure that nickname was all hype. I remember weeks after that Series, at the winter meetings in December of that year, our people still were terribly, terribly disappointed. I remember the look on Frank Cashen's face, and Jerry Hoffberger's. It was awful. Down deep, they—hell, all of us—still didn't feel the Mets were capable of beating us.

What hurt was that we helped them do it. Harry Dalton didn't guess as well this time as he had in 1966. Early in September, Harry said, "We're going to have to start following some of these ballclubs. There's no way the Mets are going to win this thing. Jim, why don't you follow Atlanta?"

So I saw the Mets exactly three games—when they swept the playoffs from Atlanta. I think one of our other guys saw three more Mets games, so we did our scouting from a total of six games. Granted, I did see the Mets a few other times in my regular duty covering the National League for trades. But doing that, and doing a World Series report on how to pitch to various players is altogether different. You can't do both at the same time, because you're gearing your mind for something entirely different.

So, going into the Series, I was a little uneasy about how little information we had on the Mets, but, truthfully, not too uneasy. We had a hell of a club—109 wins, we won our division by 19 games, we had just swept Minnesota in the American League playoffs. OK, so Tom Seaver was outstanding, but the second pitch he threw in that 1969 World Series Don Buford knocked out of the ballpark and we beat him behind Mike Cuellar, 4-1. So we're past Seaver, we're up by a game—it looked right then like it would take a miracle to beat us. And one was on order.

Cuellar, the one I considered my steal, won 23 games for us that year. Before the Series, Leonard Koppett, the *New York Times'* baseball man, interviewed me and asked, "What do you tell those pitchers?" "With each batter," I told him, "there are several things to know: Is he a high- or a low-ball hitter? Does he pull the ball or use the whole field? Is he a threat to bunt, or drag a bunt? Is he a good cripple hitter, on 3-0 or 3-1? Will he chase a bad pitch with two strikes? Does he shorten his swing with two strikes? Does he guess area on a pitch? Where is his power zone? Where is the best place to throw him a fastball? Does he want to extend his arms? Is he a first-ball hitter or will he take the first pitch? That's part of it."

And then I said, "We don't say much at all to Cuellar." He asked why not.

"He's an artist," I said. "They don't tell Leonard Bernstein how to conduct the New York Philharmonic. We don't tell Cuellar how to pitch."

Leonard—Koppett, not Bernstein—liked that.

Still, I wasn't particularly proud of the report I had on the Mets.

For example, the only time I saw Gary Gentry pitch that season was in a playoff game, and he didn't throw the ball very well. My report told our players he had an average major league fastball. He worked the third game of the Series against us, a critical game in a Series that was tied 1-1, and just threw the hell out of the ball. It was Palmer-Koufax in reverse; Palmer lost this time in a 5-0 shutout.

I felt terrible that day. A couple of our players afterward said, "I thought you said he didn't throw hard"—not sarcastically, just surprised because I think by then they had grown to have some confidence in the reports they were getting. But Red Foley, a *New York Daily News* sportswriter, came up to me afterward and said, "I've seen Gentry a lot of times and that's the hardest I've ever seen him throw this year."

I guess the adrenalin was flowing. But Gentry never was a

slop thrower. That day he pitched the first 6 2/3 innings and left with a 4-0 lead and the bases loaded, turning it over to a young relief pitcher who gave us just one single the rest of the way. A kid named Nolan Ryan.

The other report from that Series that stands out in my mind was one that never happened.

I was in front of the players, going through the names and discussing the information with them, when I came to:

"Al Weis...some of us know him from the American League, and..."

At that point, Earl Weaver jumped up and said, "Wait a minute. Just throw the God-damned ball right down the middle of the plate with that guy. Don't piss around with him. Understand? Let's go to the next guy."

I couldn't blame him. Weis had come up with the White Sox and played mostly as a backup infielder—switch-hitter, very skinny, sort of the prototype of good-field, no-hit, at least no-power. He had three home runs in six years with them.

But remember this was 1969, the Year of the Miracle Mets. Al Weis led both teams in the Series with a .455 batting average. He won Game 2 for the Mets with a two-out single in the ninth. Then, with our club down 3-1 in games but ahead 3-2 in the fifth game, Dave McNally just threw the God-damned ball right down the middle of the plate and Weis hit it out of the ballpark.

I don't think Earl ever interrupted me on a scouting report again.

Truthfully, as a manager Earl hadn't matured by that time. He was still going after umpires when he should have had his mind on what he wanted to do in the game. He got much better in the latter stages of his career.

The umpires—that was a different story. I'm not sure they improved as much as Earl did. An incident in that 1969 World Series illustrated the fact that these guys who are usually given credit for almost superhuman qualities of objectivity and fairness have their pettiness, too.

The fourth game was a hell of a big game—Mets up two games to one, their best, Seaver, working against our best,

Cuellar, at Shea Stadium. If we win it, the Series is tied, and two of the last three games will be at our place. And, dammit, we've got the better team.

Shag Crawford of the National League was working behind the plate. Our players were on him from the bench for his balls and strikes calls, and Crawford theatrically pointed his finger at one of them. I wasn't in there, of course, but I've heard from enough guys whose word I trust that in trying to defend his ballplayers, Weaver asked from the top step of the dugout: "What did he say? What did he say, Shag?"

And Crawford threw him out of the game. Technically, you aren't allowed to do what Earl did, but this was a World Series game, for Christ's sake.

Elrod Hendricks was our catcher that day, and our guys told me later that when he took his position the next inning, Crawford bragged to him, "I said I was gonna get him and I got him."

I consider myself a great friend of umpires. Our lines of work put each of us on the road a lot, and our paths crossed a lot in restaurants, or maybe I would drop in to talk with them before a game. I liked a lot of them, and I may even have been responsible for some of them being in the league. I always wrote the American League office when I saw a good umpire working in the minor leagues.

I'm an American Leaguer to the bone, but umpiring is the one area where I give the National League an edge. It isn't just me, either. Through the years, I made it a habit—out of personal curiosity more than anything else—to talk to players who went from one league to the other. You always hear so much about differences between the leagues, but from players who actually made the switch the one consistent difference I kept hearing about was quality of umpiring. Not just a majority of the time, always the edge came out for the National League.

Both of them have been slow to correct one major weakness: their method for selection of umpires for post-season play. The system advances the best teams to the playoffs and World Series, but that's not the way it works for umpires. They get those jobs on a rotation basis: "It's your turn Joe, Jim, John,

Frank, Charlie and Harry—you go to the playoffs. And Bill, Bob and Benny get the Series.''

Dammit, that's wrong. Post-season assignments should be a reward for being the best, as the newest contract with the umpires (1991) seems to be suggesting. Now, it would be even better if they would go a step further and recognize that some outstanding base umpires are very mediocre plate umpires and confine plate umpiring to a special few. That number would not include, for example, Durwood Merrill of the American League. Durwood is an outstanding base umpire; I'd want him working every post-season game I could. But you can tell from the way he works *he* knows he's not a good ball-and-strikes man. Why put him in that position?

My list of post-season plate umpires also would not include Terry Cooney, who I feel was justified in throwing out Roger Clemens in the 1990 American League playoffs but only because Cooney let things deteriorate to the place where he almost had to do it. I sat at home and watched, and my feeling was that what was being demonstrated there was along the lines of a cartoon I once saw: a psychiatrist saying to a patient, ''No, Mr. Smith, you don't have an inferiority complex—you *are* inferior.'' I think Cooney knew he had made some mistakes, but the rules of baseball make him above criticism—which meant that he was within his rights in cracking down on Clemens, who may have been right that Cooney was wrong on some calls but was wrong in pointing it out. Follow that one all the way through and you might understand why a Clemens, or an Earl Weaver, occasionally goes off the deep end.

Balls-and-strikes calls always will be baseball's vulnerability. In general, the American League has a higher strike zone, but even there it bears no resemblance to the rulebook. I was going to breakfast in Boston one day and ran into Dick Butler, who was head of American League umpires at the time. I must have been in an ornery mood, because I said, ''Dick, I'm about to call a report to Earl on the Rangers, and there are some guys on that team I'd like to pitch 'up.' Can you tell me just exactly how high we can go with that and still get a called strike?''

He said, "Why, between the shoulders and the knees."

Honest to God, that's what he said—just what we used to say it was on the sandlots. Anyone who has seen a game in the last twenty years knows the high strike has come down and down until it's about the waist now, but that's what Butler told me. Then he said, "There's [umpire] Jerry Neudecker over there. Ask him."

I liked Jerry, and I did ask him. He hemmed and hawed and finally said, "No two umpires are alike. We all have our strike zone."

I said, "Jerry, is that the best you can be? I've got to call a report to Earl in Texas."

He said, "Aw, what the hell's the difference? They're not going to throw it where you want it anyhow."

I think what all those players who played in the two leagues were telling me was that the National League at least *had* a strike zone.

Conversation with umpires does give you a different view of just what goes on in games. But every now and then, Weaver's name would come up and one of the umpires in the crew would say something like: "I had that little SOB in B-ball. He did this and he did that." And that would upset me. I'd say, "Wait a minute. That's not right. When the game is over, you're supposed to forget all that stuff. One of Earl's strengths—and he has a few strengths—is that he never carries a grudge, and I hear you guys bringing up things seven years later."

And here's Shag Crawford doing exactly that kind of thing—unprofessional as hell, in my opinion—and in a crucial World Series game. Maybe the versions I've heard underplay what Weaver did, but I don't think so. You don't have to do a hell of a lot to an umpire who'd say, "I said I'm gonna get him and I got him."

And maybe it's a good thing he did, because we might not have left that ballpark for a while that day. The game went into the tenth inning tied 1-1, and it ended with J.C. Martin trying to bunt the winning run over to third with nobody out. Pete Richert picked up the bunt and his throw to first hit Martin in the wrist and deflected past Davey Johnson at first base all the way into right field, the winning run scoring on the play. Every film I've ever seen of that game shows that it hit Martin because he was running inside the baseline, which means it should have been an interference call, with Martin out and the runners returning to first and second. Billy Hunter was acting manager, because Earl had been run out, and he didn't say anything about it—no one did. I'll guarantee you Earl Weaver would have.

And, by the way, it was Shag Crawford's call.

One other thing about that game: Donn Clendenon hit a second-inning homer off Cuellar and Seaver took that 1-0 lead into the ninth inning. We've *got* to win that game, and Seaver is just throwing an outstanding game protecting that lead. But with one out in the ninth, our reliables came up. Frank Robinson singled; Boog Powell singled him to third; Brooks came up and shot a ball into rightfield. . .but the Mets' rightfielder, not much of a defensive player, came running in, slid across the outfield on his ass, and made a remarkable catch that saved the game. The tying run did score after the catch, but that's all we got from a situation that could have been much bigger, if that rightfielder had done as almost any other outfielder of the day and played it safe. And damned if the same guy didn't end the inning by making a good running catch of a drive by Elrod Hendricks.

The rightfielder was Ron Swoboda, the Baltimore-area kid we almost took when Jim Palmer was available. And in the fifth game, right after the Weis homer that tied the game, Swoboda's double drove in Cleon Jones with what became the winning run.

So rightfielder Swoboda and second baseman Weis were two of the Miracle Mets' heroes in that Series, and there it was in my Series report: ''. . .below-average at second and right field.'' And I was right. Maybe what happened truly was a miracle.

That Swoboda catch on Brooks Robinson, incidentally, became one of the most famous scenes from that Series. I may be wrong, but it seems to me it reshaped baseball. Almost any other outfielder would have played that safe, but he slides in and makes that catch. I don't ever recall outfielders making that play that way before, sliding on their fanny but still upright, in position to get a glove under a ball just above the grass. That was a diving play before, but since Swoboda robbed Brooks Robinson with World Series exposure, it has become a rather common technique. In every night's highlights, they're sliding halfway across the outfield and they've got that ball in the webbing, making great catches all over the place.

And I'll go to my dying day convinced the play that they're all patterning after was an accident. I'd swear he came in too fast and too far to make the "right" play, fell on his ass, slid to the right spot, came up with the catch—and invented a new way to play short fly balls.

And I'm still glad we took Jim Palmer.

I never want to give the impression of shortchanging those Miracle Mets. Yes, I think the Orioles were a better ballclub, but the Mets went out and won that Series and deserve all the credit in the world for it. I'd also have to say we lost and we shouldn't have. We committed what, to a scout, is a cardinal sin. We weren't properly prepared, and I have to blame that on Harry Dalton's decision to concentrate on Atlanta rather than the Mets in our September scouting.

I have to smile when I reread the report I gave to our players:

"Don't sell this club short. Everything they have been doing lately has been working for them. They have great spirit and hustle. They think they are a Team of Destiny. Let's put an end to this foolish thinking."

Still, it's never a baseball miracle when pitching prevails, and the Mets did have those wonderful arms: Tom Seaver, Jerry Koosman, and that kid who hadn't even cracked their starting rotation, Nolan Ryan.

The day in 1991 when Ryan, at forty-four, pitched his seventh no-hit game, I was stirred and excited and pleased as was everyone else who admires grace and greatness. By coincidence, it was the day Rickey Henderson finally got around Lou Brock to claim the career base-stealing record. The contrast between Rickey's cockiness and Ryan's humility certainly gave that round to yesterday's generation over today's.

There was Henderson, on the field, into national microphones, with the game stopped and Brock standing beside him, for Christ's sake, saying: "Lou Brock was a great base-stealer . . . but today I'm the greatest of all time."

And there was Ryan, *three* no-hitters beyond the great Sandy Koufax, finishing off his no-hitter with an old-fashioned high hard one that simply overpowered one of today's best young players, Roberto Alomar . . . walking off the mound with a grin and a handshake for his catcher . . . taking the time to give all the interviews necessary . . . and then finishing the evening the way he has disciplined himself to do every time: in a weight room, working out.

It made me curious. I went to my files and dug out my World Series report on Nolan Ryan:

"Very good to excellent fastball, Palmer-type when Palmer is at his best. Doesn't control curve well, uses it when ahead. Tendency to be wild at times."

Later on, from the card file I maintained from year to year on players from both leagues that we might consider trying to acquire:

1980—"Fastball 7 [8, you'll remember, is the best—I didn't even put him up there], just an average curve ball."

1981—"Fastball 8, curve 7 [well above average], change curve 6, straight change 6 . . . quick move to first, but you can get a jump on his delivery." We had a line on our questionnaire: Can he help us? Remember, we had a pretty good ballclub; we had just been to the Series in 1979. I said no, a qualified no. "Yes, he can help us, but we can't afford his contract."

1982—"Fastball 8, curve 7 but not consistent . . . when he misses with it early, he abandons it."

Two things struck me after looking at those reports: 1) even in throwing that seventh no-hitter, the part about the curve ball still was true; he had a real good one early in the game, then lost control with it and went almost entirely to his fastball; and 2) among the many amazing things about him is that he has continued to get better and better and better as a pitcher. Remember, it was only a few years ago, even after he had passed Koufax's record for no-hitters, that people said he shouldn't make the Hall of Fame because he was just a .500 pitcher. After seven no-hitters and more than 5,000 strikeouts, nobody's saying that any more. Either he's getting better or we're getting smarter, and either way, he's responsible for making it happen.

Some people thought we brought our own miracle with us in the 1970 World Series.

He wore No. 5.

I've seen a lot of baseball and I've never seen anybody put the whole game together as absolutely brilliantly over a significant period of time as Brooks Robinson did in the 1970 World Series.

Now, the truth is that all of those amazing plays that Brooks made at third base in that Series were not very far out of what we had grown to expect as the ordinary from him. I've made it abundantly clear how I feel about what Frank Robinson gave us when he joined us in 1966. We already had Brooks then, and putting the two stars together didn't diminish either one, as it can when egos get involved, but rather brought out even better things from both. When Earl Weaver and I would have one of those sessions where we were going at each other as only two guys with enormous respect for the other one can, I used to say, "Yeah, you're a great manager, Earl. And I'll tell you when you became great: The day you learned how to write 'Robinson' on your lineup card...twice."

I could have retired several years earlier than I did if I'd have had $100 for every time somebody came up to me at a ballpark or in a hotel lobby or bar or restaurant and said, "I saw Brooks in a game on TV last night and you wouldn't believe the play he made."

I'd just smile, because I knew I'd probably seen a hundred just like it. He did that throughout his entire career. We'd watch and we'd grin but we wouldn't even get excited about plays that other third basemen would love to have made, just once.

But even I have to admit that Brooks Robinson in that 1970 Series was extraordinary. Extra-HIS-ordinary.

You have to remember who we were playing. I loved our ballclub, and I had a lot of respect for the Oakland ballclubs that came along right after our peak years with the Robinsons and did something we never did: win three straight World Series. And, of course, there were a lot of great Yankee teams, the best of my years probably the Mantle and Maris teams of the early 1960s.

But from the other league, in all my years of watching I never saw a club that impressed me more than those Cincinnati "Big Red Machine" teams of the 1970s. I don't think any of those other teams I mentioned, including ours, could match the day-to-day, eight-man lineup those Reds teams had. I think all of those other ones had better pitching—if the Reds had an Achilles' heel, that was it. Pitching is so important to the game you'd have to give those Yankees, A's and Orioles teams an overall edge over the Reds teams. But for a combination of hitting, power, defense, speed, everything vital to the game but pitching—no team I saw could match those Reds teams.

In 1970, we caught them on their way up. They still hadn't made their trade that raised them to the final level of excellence: essentially Lee May for Joe Morgan, which was one damned good player for another who got to Cincinnati and blossomed into a Hall of Famer. What made it such a good trade for the Reds was that even a couple of fringe players in that deal, centerfielder Cesar Geronimo and pitcher Jack Billingham, became big contributors to their success, too.

If Lee May hadn't still been in Cincinnati in 1970, though, Brooks Robinson might have had just a routinely terrific series. May, Johnny Bench and Tony Perez were three powerful right-handed hitters who made third base the worst position in the world to play against them, unless you were Brooks Robinson.

That whole 1970 Series was just one long string of bullets one of those power guys tried to blast past Brooks. It hasn't worked yet. He dived to his left, to his right, straight up in the air—I swear he threw May out one time from behind the third-base coach after diving to make a backhanded stop of a shot down the line. Or maybe it was Bench. Or Perez. By now, it's just a beautiful, memorable blend.

And the guy also was dynamic at the plate: nine hits (.429), six RBI, two homers. His homer in the seventh off Gary Nolan won us the first game, 4-3. His bases-loaded double in the first got us rolling in the third game that we won 9-3. The only game we lost he went 4-for-4 trying to pull it out.

And the last inning of the last game was an appropriate ending:

Bench lined to Brooks.

Mike Cuellar struck out May.

Pat Corrales grounded to Brooks.

Perfect.

But I had tremendous respect for the Reds.

Preparing a scouting report on that team had been a real challenge. After Brooks Robinson's great Series, it may sound a little phony, but we really did want to make them hit the ball on the ground—because of Brooks *and* the rest of our outstanding infield.

But there was a bit of a problem in that: we had never played on artificial turf, and Cincinnati's new stadium had it.

I was concerned. In scouting the Reds, I noticed they wore shoes with hard rubber cleats. We wore the standard spikes. Well ahead of the Series, I called our general manager, Harry Dalton, and discussed the situation with him. The world championship was at stake; it was no time to give away even the slightest advantage.

Harry bought new shoes with rubber cleats for all our players. It turned out that some wore them and some stuck with their regular spiked shoes. Harry let me know after the Series that it had cost the club $1,500 for those new shoes and they really weren't necessary.

A young Jim Russo dazzles them as sports director of KPRO in Riverside, California. It wasn't long before the traffic manager at the station, a lovely young lady who later became my wife, was dazzling me.

My first signee ever. Vachel Perkins was 18 years old when I signed him in 1949. He became the top prospect in the Browns organization but was forced to retire in 1954 with a bad arm before he reached the majors.

This scouting trip to Nicaragua in 1962 to look at Dave Nicholson was the only time my wife, Betty, got irritated with the demands of my job. Maybe she knew something; we traded Nicholson a month later.

Coach Bob Knight joined me in spring training in 1981 after his Indiana squad won the NCAA Basketball Championship. Bob is a great baseball fan and I've been lucky enough to count him as one of my friends for the last 18 years.

My five children help me celebrate at my retirement party in 1987. They are, left to right, Ron, Nancy, Cliff, Susan and Jennifer. I'm the one dressed in black about to cry.

Bucky Dent (left) and Greg Riddoch (right) help me celebrate my induction into the Greater St. Louis Baseball Scouts Hall of Fame in August 1991.

Jerry Hoffberger was the ultimate owner.
Morale and the Oriole tradition were at
their height during his ownership. And he
brewed the best damned beer in the
country—National Premium. *(Courtesy
Baltimore Orioles)*

Edward Bennett Williams
owned the Orioles from
1979 to 1988. He
increased attendance by
spending more on
promotions and setting up
an Orioles office in
Washington, D.C., for
ticket sales. *(Courtesy
Baltimore Orioles)*

Though William O. DeWitt,
Jr., never owned the
Orioles, he is a part of
their history. He and his
brother owned the Browns
when I first joined the
team, and he was the
owner of the Reds when
the Orioles acquired Frank
Robinson. A helluva
baseball man.

I got to know Bill Veeck
when he was the owner of
the St. Louis Browns.
Highly intelligent, Bill was
a friend to all fans. What I
wouldn't give for one last
chance to sit with him in
the Bards' Room at
Comiskey Park and talk
about baseball and life.
(Courtesy Chicago White Sox)

Tim McCarver had a good career with the Cardinals, Phillies, Red Sox and Expos before he went on to an even better broadcasting career. In 1959, I was all set to make Tim an offer out of high school, but I refused to talk to him with his "adviser" present. *(Courtesy Philadelphia Phillies/Paul Roedig)*

An early Oriole prospect, Fred Valentine was a favorite of mine. A fine person and a real talent, he was mishandled in the minors and didn't find success until he was with the Washington Senators. *(Courtesy Baltimore Orioles)*

Rogers Hornsby's personality didn't match his prowess as a player. If he represents the best of sports' Golden Age, I'll take today's athletes and attitudes. *(Courtesy St. Louis Post-Dispatch)*

Three members of the "Kiddie Korps" from the late 1950s and early 1960s: Chuck Estrada (left), Jerry Walker (center), Jack Fisher (right). *(Courtesy Baltimore Orioles/Tadder)*

You have to give quality to receive quality. Milt Pappas was our top pitcher in 1965, but I argued long and hard for the trade that sent him, Jack Baldschun and Dick Simpson to Cincinnati for Frank Robinson. *(Courtesy Baltimore Orioles/Tadder)*

Frank Robinson was responsible for turning the Orioles into winners. He had great instincts and talent, and knew how to lead. *(Courtesy Baltimore Orioles)*

The best pitcher in Orioles history. Injuries were the only thing that prevented Jim Palmer from winning 300 games. His verbal clashes with Earl Weaver are legendary. *(Courtesy Baltimore Orioles)*

Brooks Robinson was a great third baseman, and a perfect Oriole. Some players would have resented another star like Frank Robinson being added to the team, but not Brooks. Together he and Frank took the Orioles to a new height. *(Courtesy Baltimore Orioles)*

Moe Drabowsky's relief effort in the first game of the 1966 World Series set the stage for the Orioles' sweep of the Dodgers. *(Courtesy Baltimore Orioles)*

Hall of Famer Don Drysdale was a great competitor who was not afraid to brush back a batter. Orioles fans remember him as the man who gave up back-to-back home runs to Frank and Brooks Robinson in Game 1 of the 1966 World Series. *(Courtesy Los Angeles Dodgers/Brent Shyer)*

Sandy Koufax was the other ace on the 1966 Dodgers. The best left-hander in modern-day baseball, when he pitched it meant 15,000 extra fans. *(Courtesy Los Angeles Dodgers/Brent Shyer)*

The Orioles began their ascent to the top when Luis Aparicio was acquired from the White Sox in January 1963. I like to think my lobbying with the writers helped Looie get into the Hall of Fame, though he earned it on his own. *(Courtesy Baltimore Orioles)*

Mark Belanger was an outstanding defensive shortstop with the Orioles from 1965 to 1981. Not much with the bat, he wouldn't bunt or drag for base hits to help his average. He managed to hit Nolan Ryan well, though. *(Courtesy Baltimore Orioles)*

The Gentle Giant. The Orioles got first baseman Boog Powell on a coin toss. He hit 303 home runs while in an Orioles uniform. *(Courtesy Baltimore Orioles/Tadder)*

When we found out that Dave Johnson wasn't going to return to Texas A&M, we moved quickly to sign him. He and Mark Belanger made as good a double play combo as there was in baseball. *(Courtesy Baltimore Orioles/Tadder)*

Roberto Clemente dominated the Orioles in the 1971 World Series with a .414 average. He always felt the media downgraded him as a player, and he used the Series to showcase his great talent. *(Courtesy Pittsburgh Pirates)*

Willie Stargell was the regular season co-MVP, the MVP in the N.L. Playoffs, and the World Series MVP all in 1979. One of the nicest guys in baseball, he had his own private reward system for friends: a gold star. It was a special moment for me when he honored me with one. *(Courtesy Pittsburgh Pirates)*

One of the greatest starting rotations in baseball history. From left to right are Mike Cuellar, Pat Dobson, Dave McNally, and Jim Palmer. They each won 20 games or more for the 1971 Orioles. I signed Jim and Dave, and recommended the trades that brought us Mike and Pat. *(Courtesy Baltimore Orioles/Tadder)*

Earl Weaver's managerial debut changed the course of the Orioles. A top manager, he knew the rule book better than most umpires. Our arguments would fill three books, but he never held a grudge. *(Courtesy Baltimore Orioles/Jerry Wachter)*

Bill Veeck gave Tony LaRussa his first managing job when he owned the White Sox. Tony is always thinking of ways to get an edge. Though not every idea has worked, enough have that he won a World Series in Oakland. *(Courtesy Oakland Athletics/Jay Alves)*

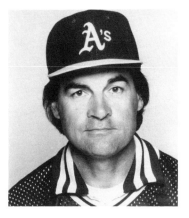

Whitey Herzog is a master at adapting his managing style to the type of ballclub he has. *(Courtesy St. Louis Cardinals/Steven Goldstein)*

Walter Alston was one of the best. His Dodger teams were always well schooled in the fundamentals of the game. *(Courtesy Los Angeles Dodgers/Brent Shyer)*

Sparky Anderson, who has made it to the World Series with the Big Red Machine and the Tigers, is excellent as far as running a ballgame. *(Courtesy Detroit Tigers)*

Billy Martin was a good strategist, but he didn't meet the extra criteria to make my top group of managers. A great competitor, Billy's happiest days might have been as the manager of the Twins. *(Courtesy New York Yankees)*

The architect of the Orioles' early
success, Paul Richards, was both
general manager and manager. He
was promised an open checkbook
when he arrived in 1955 and he
took full advantage of it. *(Courtesy
Baltimore Orioles)*

Jim McLaughlin was the
scouting and farm director
during the Paul Richards years.
Jim's feud with Paul, and the
splitting of the scouting
department into two factions
caused by it (I was a
McLaughlin man), was
detrimental to the overall
success of the Orioles.
(Courtesy Baltimore Orioles/Tadder)

Frank Cashen was adept at
looking at and analyzing the
whole picture. I believe the
downfall of the Orioles was
when Frank was moved to the
brewery and Hank Peters took
over baseball operations.
(Courtesy Baltimore Orioles/Tadder)

I told Earl he should open the 1979 World Series against the Pirates with a lefty. My choice was Scott McGregor (left), but Earl went with Mike Flanagan (right). *(Courtesy Baltimore Orioles/Jerry Wachter)*

We obtained Ken Singleton (left) and Mike Torrez (right) from the Expos in the Dave McNally deal. Singleton could hit blindfolded, and Torrez won 20 games for us in 1975. *(Courtesy Baltimore Orioles)*

Steve Dalkowski might have been the hardest thrower I ever saw, but he could never make it to the majors. His first year in the minors he struck out 121 batters in 62 innings, and walked 129. *(Courtesy Baltimore Orioles)*

Dennis Martinez always had the stuff to be a winner, but alcohol sidetracked him for awhile. What a thrill to see him get it all together and pitch a perfect game against the Dodgers in 1991. *(Courtesy Montreal Expos/Richard Griffin)*

Future Hall of Famer Mike Schmidt came right out of my scouting heartland and we missed him. We faced him and the Phillies in the 1983 World Series and thankfully handled Mike pretty well (1-for-20). *(Courtesy Philadelphia Phillies/Al Tielemans)*

Dave McNally had four straight 20-win seasons for us. When traded to Montreal, he retired during the season because he didn't want to take the Expo's money if he couldn't get the hitters out. *(Courtesy Baltimore Orioles/Jay Spencer)*

Though he had a short career in Baltimore, Tito Landrum will always be remembered by O's fans for his dramatic tenth-inning home run to defeat the White Sox in the 1983 playoffs. *(Courtesy Baltimore Orioles)*

I consider my scouting of Mike Cuellar to be one of my two best. From 1969 to 1972, he was our top pitcher, recording 85 wins. *(Courtesy Baltimore Orioles)*

Cal Ripken, Jr.'s attitude and his great ability will take him to the Hall of Fame. When he first came up, I suggested that we move Cal to third base because the rigors of playing shortstop could be tough on a man his size. *(Courtesy Baltimore Orioles)*

When Nolan Ryan threw his seventh no-hitter, I was as excited and pleased as anyone. Rickey Henderson broke Lou Brock's base-stealing record on the same day, but there was a world of difference in the way they each handled their success. *(Courtesy Texas Rangers/John Blake)*

In 1982, when I helped the Cardinals prepare their arbitration case against Ozzie Smith, he was a top defensive shortstop. The Cardinals won the case and saved $300,000, but Ozzie improved his hitting and eventually cost the Cards a lot more. *(Courtesy St. Louis Cardinals)*

We'll never know. But I do know if we hadn't spent the money and our footing on the artificial turf had cost us the Series, $1,500 would have looked pretty tiny. To me, it was just the kind of detail work a scout is paid to do. I even asked and got permission from the Reds, on one of my visits to Riverfront Stadium, to walk on the field and bounce a baseball on this newfangled artificial stuff so I could get the feel of it. The primary opinion I formed was that I didn't like it, because it certainly affects the game—especially outfield play. The turf became more and more common, but I never changed that opinion.

Nor did I lower my respect for the Reds, even after our four-to-one Series victory.

The last game was at our place, and we had the usual locker room celebration. I remember coming out of the stadium after that, and the Reds' bus was still sitting at the curb, with most of the players on it. I took a little chance; there I was, soaked, champagne all over me, and I sure didn't want to come across to them like a gloating winner, but I just felt obligated to tell them how impressed I was after all the time I had watched them that September in getting our report ready.

So, I got on that bus and I told them: how well I thought they had played, and that I thought we had beaten a hell of a ballclub. I also told them I wasn't real sure that the best team had won, and I meant it. It was a good ballclub, obviously, and we had just had a real good Series.

Especially No. 5.

Pittsburgh was a fish we never could land, but I sure thought we had 'em hooked. Twice.

I have too much respect for the game to ever use the word fluke in connection with a team that won the World Series. Way too much had to go into a six-month effort for that word to apply, but I would have to say if ever a World Series outcome bordered on being fluky, it was the 1960 Series that Bill Mazeroski won for the Pirates with a ninth-inning, seventh-game home run. The Pirates that year won their games 6-4, 3-2, 5-2 and 10-9;

the Yankees, with Mantle, Maris, Skowron, Howard, Berra, Ford—and Stengel, won theirs 16-3, 10-0 and 12-0. To this day, the World Series records for runs scored in a Series (55) *and* for the biggest difference in runs over the opponent (28) are held by that Yankee team that lost.

Compared with that, maybe we don't really have a complaint about the seven-game Series losses we had to the Pirates in both 1971 and 1979, but that didn't make them feel any better.

In 1971, we should have been making our bid for three in a row, but the loss to the Miracle Mets in 1969 ruled that out. Still, I think we were pretty well accepted as the dominant team in the game when we went over 100 wins for the third straight year (no record, but the Ruth-Gehrig Yankee teams, the DiMaggio teams, the Mantle-Maris teams, none of those ever did that), and we swept the league playoffs for the third straight year (no other team has ever done that). We felt pretty confident opening against Pittsburgh in 1971, and all the more so after winning the first two games.

I'm not sure we ever got Roberto Clemente out again after that. The record book says we did, but I sure don't remember it.

In retrospect, I'm almost glad it happened the way it did. . . which is stretching almost about as far as it can be stretched. Obviously, I'd have rather won—without a doubt. But the years have mellowed me enough to see some beauty in the fact that Roberto Clemente was so great in getting the job done, right up to the seventh-game home run that made the difference in a 2-1 game. He had 12 hits in that Series—I'll admit it, I had no secrets to pass along on how or where to pitch him because his hitting zone wasn't even limited to the strike zone.

Just over a year later, Roberto Clemente was dead—killed in a plane crash on a humanitarian flight taking supplies to storm-ravaged Managua, Nicaragua. Vaya con dios, Roberto. If we had to lose. . .

Even now, I can't find anything cheerful about losing in 1979. That one really hurt.

We were an entirely different team by then. The Robinsons had moved on, and the Yankee trade had reloaded our pitching staff to where we were ready to begin another pretty rich era. We still had Jim Palmer, but he wasn't the kid on a staff with Dave McNally and Mike Cuellar. He was the veteran with new guys named Mike Flanagan, Scott McGregor and Dennis Martinez.

Pittsburgh wasn't bad. Willie Stargell had the year that clinched Hall of Fame membership for him. That year, he was MVP in the regular season, the playoffs and the World Series. He did have to share MVP for the season that year with Keith Hernandez of the Cardinals, but that's still a Triple Crown that nobody else has matched. Not many ever matched Willie Stargell the man, either. He had his own, private reward system: he would award a little gold star to friends of his when he thought they had earned one. One day he gave me one, and I'll guarantee you it was a very special moment for me.

It was primarily because of Willie and Dave Parker that I had made the recommendation to Earl Weaver that he open with a left-hander—McGregor in my mind, Flanagan in Earl's. I liked Flanagan, too—he was the Cy Young Award winner that year. But my preference for McGregor was that I thought his off-speed pitches would give that big, powerful, free-swinging Pirates team the most trouble.

We had a pretty good young right-hander on that team. Dennis Martinez was just twenty-four, but he led us in innings pitched that year and won 15 games. He almost won the third playoff game against the Angels, leaving in the ninth with a 3-2 lead and Rod Carew on second base. Don Stanhouse came on in relief and never got anybody out, so Dennis didn't get a W and we had to wait a day to close out our championship.

As things turned out, maybe we should have given Martinez a chance in that 1979 Series. Right-handed and all, he did have outstanding stuff. He always did have. That was never his problem. He had some troubles with his arm, but his biggest battle was with alcoholism, and I've always been sympathetic with him on that score because I know some of the background. He was from Nicaragua, and when things started getting rough down there, with guerrilla warfare in the streets and the country torn apart by revolution, he tried to get his mother out. You'd think the first baseball player to come from there and make it big in the major leagues would have been enough of a hero in that baseball-loving country to have some pull, but that little nation was so divided then that nobody had good connections. It became a desperate thing with Dennis, fearing for his mother's safety, and I've always felt that contributed to his problems.

It got tough for him. His performance fell off, and people in our organization wanted to dump him. I believe in discipline as much as anyone does. Ordinarily, I'd probably have been for getting rid of a problem, too. But Dennis Martinez is a nice person—and a hell of a pitcher. We did keep him a while, and one of the years when he seemed to be getting it back together, he came up to me in spring training with tears in his eyes and thanked me for standing up for him. He said, "Mr. Russo, I'm dedicating this season to my mother and to you."

So let me tell you, it was an awfully big night for me, all those years later, when I was sitting in my home late on a summer night in 1991 watching the ESPN pictures out of Los Angeles, and seeing thirty-six-year-old Dennis Martinez complete the rarity of rarities—a perfect game. Dennis was so overcome after the third out the camera showed him in tears when his teammates mobbed him. I shed a few of those right then, too. What a hell of a performance, and a hell of an answer to people who gave up on him.

I can't say I fought too hard to get him in against those 1979 Pirates. I did lobby some for using Steve Stone in that Series, even though he was right-handed. I was a year too early to convince Earl with that one. Stone the next season had as good a year as a curve ball pitcher can have. He was an artist all year long and won 25 games, the only time anyone did that in the 1980s. If you ever want the term "career year" defined, do it with Steve Stone 1980. He could throw a curve ball for strikes any time he wanted to, anywhere he wanted to, and it was a real good curve ball. He had a fantastic year.

And he was out of baseball a year later. Bad arm.

I read one time where Steve was quoted as saying he didn't

"take Jimmy Russo too seriously—I'm going to pitch my own ballgame." I had a hard time believing Steve said that, because I can remember one year in spring training, we were playing the Phillies in an exhibition game, and he asked me, "What can you tell me about these guys?" Elrod Hendricks, our catcher, heard him and said, "What the hell's the difference? It's just an exhibition game." Stone said, "Anything you can learn is going to help you." So we sat down and went over a few of their hitters.

That's one reason I had trouble believing that quote—doing that in an exhibition game. And another reason has come in the years since then, with me sitting around the house and Steve Stone on TV every day with Harry Caray and the Cubs telecasts. I think most people in baseball think Steve does an outstanding job—and you know why? Because of the comments he continually makes about the right pitch to throw to this batter at this particular time, the comments that work out a high percentage of the time and stamp Steve as someone who knows not just baseball but specific batters and specific pitchers pretty well, sound like a scout, a damned good one.

I believed in him when I told Earl before that Series, "There's a possibility that Stone could give this team a little trouble," simply because they were a free-swinging club that tried to jack everything out—the perfect opponent for a guy with a little finesse. I'm sure Earl could cite from memory how Stone did pitch two innings in relief in that Series and gave up two runs. That's not like starting a game and getting fully prepared to go after a team.

And besides, only Steve and Earl probably remembered those two innings, because they got washed away in team success. They came in a game where we scored six runs in the eighth to come from behind and win, 9-6, the first of two in a row for us at Three Rivers Stadium to give us a lead of three games to one: one win away from the world championship.

And we're still that one win short.

People remember that Pirates team for its "Fam-i-lee" stuff and for Stargell's great season, but what I remember is how in that Series' last three games, every move that Chuck

Tanner made as manager of the Pirates worked out great, including some that looked pretty questionable to me at the time—and every move by Earl Weaver, a pretty shrewd manager, worked out awful, including some that looked right to me at the time.

When we went back to Baltimore with a 3-2 lead, the writers set up a press conference on the off-day not with the two managers but, as kind of a change of pace, with the two scouts who had written "The Book" on the two clubs: Lennie Yochim and me.

It was fun. The writers were firing questions at us and I was enjoying it, but I was always pretty careful what I said in situations like that—like a college coach wary of saying something that his opponent could put on the locker room wall for psychological purposes.

Even though we were a game up, the Pirates had hit our pitching for a .339 average in those first five games, and I was asked if I was surprised by that. I said, "No, I'm not surprised. This is the Pittsburgh Pirates. We're not playing the Monongahela Sunday All-Stars. This is a good ballclub.

"We're not hitting, but I think in baseball you have to give the other guy credit. In this situation, Pittsburgh has good pitching and good balance.

"I think we're going to be all right. We only have one more game to win, but we have to go out and win it."

And they asked me if the Orioles were following the scouting instructions and doing what I wanted them to do.

"Oh, yeah. We're pitching them as well as we know how to pitch them. We're just not hitting the ball. Sometimes you have no control over that.

"But I think we're in a pretty good situation."

Then they asked the same question to Lennie: "Have the Pirates done the things that you've wanted them to do?"

He just smiled and said:

"Only in the games we've won."

In all the press conferences I've listened in on, that was one of the best answers I've heard.

"Only in the games we've won."

That was great.

The rest of the Series wasn't.

The Earl Weaver era was over when we made our next—and my last—appearance in the World Series.

Earl had retired at the end of the 1982 season, and Joe Altobelli moved up from coach to replace him. Joe was a very moody person. One minute he was smiling, the next he sulked. He and Earl were never close. Joe wanted Earl's job.

But when he got it, he was smart enough to know he was taking over a pretty good ballclub and for the most part he just tried to keep it going.

It made him the manager of a World Series champion, not a bad line in history. The Orioles won that 1983 Series by spotting Philadelphia a first-game victory and then blowing the Phillies away in the next four games.

Primarily I remember two things about that Series.

No. 1 was something that occurred off the field, related to us only because it showed that the development we pioneered—advance scouting for post-season play—had reached the point where it got a manager fired once, before he got to be manager.

After that 1983 World Series, one of the Phillies' coaches, Bobby Wine, was quietly let go. Inside baseball, it stunned people, because Bobby wasn't just a coach on that staff, he seemed very tight with the manager, Paul Owens, and the general manager, Bill Giles. Owens was ready to retire, everyone knew that, and Wine—an old Phillies shortstop; everyone remembers the days of Wine and Rojas (Cookie) at Philadelphia—was right there ready to take over as manager. And even when Owens was managing the ballclub, Wine was calling the shots.

So the Phillies won the pennant, and it was generally assumed Owens would retire from the dugout and move into the front office with Wine taking over the club. When spring came, Owens was still manager and Wine was gone.

The story?

Down the stretch that year, the Phillies had their scouts on us: scouting director Jack Pastore, Moose Johnson and Eddie Bockman. They worked their asses off making the report on the Orioles, and they were ready to present it.

Wine was a real close friend of Gene Mauch, who was managing California then. Before the scouts' report on our team came in, Wine called Mauch and said, "Tell me all about the Orioles." Mauch told him, and he scribbled the notes down. And when the scouts came in with their report, Wine told them not to bother, "We got all the information we need from Mauch."

Everybody was dumbfounded, from Giles on down. That was the move that cost fair-haired boy Bobby Wine not only his managing chance but his job—that move, plus our four games to one wipeout of the Phillies in the Series. If the results had been reversed, Wine might have been the manager, but he'd have had a tough time getting those scouts back.

My other memory of that Series: It was a pretty good Phillies team, with one outstanding player, Mike Schmidt. Schmidt forever was a frustration for me because he came right out of my old scouting heartland, in the period when finding players was my biggest job, and somehow this big, talented, athletic future Hall of Famer never caught the eye of anyone in our organization.

Mike was from Dayton, and he played shortstop at Ohio University—played four years there and got his degree in 1971. My early-spring job in those days was cross-checking the top thirty or thirty-five prospects in the country, and the name of Michael Jack Schmidt never did enter my files. The better he got, the more that bothered me, and one day I ran into the late Jack Baker, our scout in the Dayton area and a good one. I asked him about as gently as I could phrase it, "Were you high on Mike Schmidt?"

I thought that subject bothered me. Jack had lived with that one a lot longer than I had, and he was *really* upset. "Hell, yes," he said. "You should see the reports I sent to the front office." He was right. I should have seen those reports—or at the very least someone (Walter Shannon was our scouting director at the time) should have seen them and sent me in to check him out, but it never happened. The year the Phillies took Schmidt in the second round (right after Kansas City had taken George Brett), the Orioles used their first-round pick on a pitcher named Randy Stein, who did get up to the major leagues for a few years, but not with us.

About the time of that 1983 Series, I was chatting with Schmidt one day and had to bring up the subject that had bothered me so long. I said, "Our scout in the area is still upset, almost to the point of shedding tears, that you weren't double-checked by our organization. He said he sent in glowing reports." Mike just laughed and said: "I didn't have that kind of power in school. I wasn't followed by thirty-five or forty scouts. I didn't start hitting the ball hard till later on."

But I should have seen Mike Schmidt.

We happened to handle him pretty well in the 1983 Series— unbelievably well, really; he was 1-for-20, a single. He had 40 regular-season homers that year.

I can't take a lot of credit for that, except in the way that pitching to him fit into some basic ideas that I'd always had, and I had seen reinforced just before the Series.

Baseball had changed between our previous World Series appearances and that one in 1983. Through the 1970s, we worried primarily about winning our division, and if we were good enough to do that, we felt pretty good about our chances to get past whoever came out of the American League West—so we could afford to take a longer look at the National League teams in September.

In 1983, we didn't have that luxury. The White Sox put together a year a lot like Steve Stone's—they won their division by twenty games, breaking one of our records. It was pretty obvious that's where our primary attention had to be, if we were going to have even a chance at winning the World Series.

The main thing they had going for them was pitching. The last half of the season, LaMarr Hoyt, Richard Dotson and Floyd

Bannister were almost unhittable—and that didn't even get to the guy I respected as much as any of them, Britt Burns.

But they also had good right-handed power in the middle of their lineup with the Rookie of the Year that year, Ron Kittle, and two free-agent pickups who had helped them a lot, Carlton Fisk and Greg Luzinski.

When I stood before our players and went over the White Sox prior to the start of the playoffs, I couldn't help but notice the difference between the first time I had done something like that, in 1966, and now—when our scouting reports had become such an article of faith with our players that they actually gave me a standing ovation when I was done. Bob Verdi, the *Chicago Tribune* columnist, wrote about that—it was just a hell of a warm and flattering moment to take into my retirement years.

We instituted something new (for us) in post-season play. I communicated with our coach, Cal Ripken, Sr., by walkie-talkie from my position behind home plate—on our defensive alignments for every hitter. We beat that White Sox team in four games (it was best-of-five then, not best-of-seven as is the case now), and afterward some of their players did some grousing about our pitchers' throwing at them. Mike Boddicker gave us a big lift by shutting them out in the second game, 4-0, after Hoyt had handled us pretty easily in the first game. Boddicker was not a strikeout pitcher, but he struck out 14. He also had not hit a batter in the entire season, but he hit two in that game. The White Sox did mention that in their complaining.

Let's go back to that meeting when I gave the scouting report. I went over each player, and even though Earl wasn't there, we were still playing by his rules. Earl always wanted to know the best place to throw the fastball to each hitter. When I came to Luzinski, I said, "The best place for a fastball with him is right on his hands." I looked out and saw McGregor nodding his head—and Boddicker shaking his head. That's how scouting reports can differ, according to the player's specific abilities. We used to refer to Boddicker's "sneaky" fastball, which meant first of all that it wasn't very fast, but once in a while, if a guy was looking for a breaking ball, Boddicker could sneak the fastball in on him and get it by him.

Whatever that first reaction meant, and I interpreted it at the time as a little bit of self-doubt within Mike about his ability to throw a fastball in on power hitters, he obviously tried it and liked it. One of the two batters he hit was Luzinski, but he also ate him up the other three times he batted. Boddicker's performance was so impressive and so influential in turning the momentum of the series that he was named MVP.

But he didn't throw at anybody. You don't win games hitting people. But I can say this: If a pitcher doesn't establish his fastball inside, he's going to get hurt. The successful pitchers—Drysdale is a great example, but there are others, Larry Dierker and Bob Gibson among them—had the ability to come inside, and kind of liked to. The only successful pitcher I've ever seen who never pitched inside was Ken Holtzman. He kept everything away, and I always wondered why. My theory was he developed that technique as a young pitcher with the Cubs, pitching in Wrigley Field where the wind blows out frequently. We sure as hell didn't teach him to do it. From 1966 on, I always tried to encourage our pitchers to pitch tight—go in and out, but don't be afraid to go after those hands.

We could have offered those post-season games in 1983 as Exhibit A. Luzinski was just helpless. We stayed right in on his hands and he got two hits, one of those a bloop. Tom Paciorek, a fine right-handed hitter, said he didn't get a decent pitch to hit in the entire playoff. And then in the Series: 1-for-20 from Mike Schmidt? Not bad.

That playoff series with the White Sox came down to game 4 in Comiskey Park with us ahead, two games to one, and Storm Davis starting for us against Burns.

It was a hell of a game, 0-0 after nine. Tippy Martinez replaced Davis in the seventh for us, but Burns stayed out there in as courageous a clutch performance as I've seen. We'd get him in trouble but he'd work out, and they had their chances, too.

In the tenth, on a cold October day, the 150th pitch Britt Burns threw was driven into the upper deck—not by Eddie

Murray or Cal Ripken or any of our marquee players but by Tito Landrum, unknown.

Let me tell you how he got there.

Tito—Terry was his real name; he was from Joplin, Missouri—was an outfielder who had knocked around in the Cardinals' system for ten years, getting up to the big club a few times but never sticking. In June, the Cardinals had an injury and asked if we had anybody available—to just plug the gap, so they wouldn't have to bring a young player up from their system and risk not being able to play him every day. We offered Floyd Rayford, a journeyman player, barely adequate defensively but he could hit the ball out once in a while—great guy, played hard. We sent him to the Cards, officially, for "a player to be named later," but actually we were just doing them a favor. At the time, we didn't really need anybody and we didn't even give much thought to who we might eventually ask for.

Not long after we made the deal, I told our general manager, Hank Peters, "If we ever get down to where it's time to talk about the ballplayer from the Cardinals' side, I think we should discuss Tito Landrum." I had made a trip into Louisville to look at a player, and Tito was there. I had seen him in spring training, and I always liked him, some—good defensive player, could run and throw, a classy guy, and I thought he swung the bat well against left-handed pitching.

A couple of months go by, we've still got a player coming from the Cardinals, and August 31 is coming up, the last day for adding anybody to your roster in time to be eligible for post-season play. I was on the road, and when I called the office to talk to Hank Peters, I was told he was out. I told our secretary, Mave Berkeridge, "Please put this message on his desk: Make sure we get Landrum by August 31." He did.

He hit .317 down the stretch for us, filling in off and on. The ballplayers loved him, just a classy guy. He acted like an Oriole.

And in the tenth inning of that scoreless fourth playoff game, with Burns pitching so well and the wind blowing in, Tito—who hit left-handers pretty well—drove the ball right through that wind and off the upper-deck facade.

Tito Landrum put us in the World Series.

In the celebration after that game, I kidded him: "Tito, I knew you had some power, but I didn't know you had upper-deck power."

Ironically, that hit that forever will be remembered in Baltimore came on his last swing as an Oriole. He got into three Series games, as a pinch-runner or defensive replacement, but never got to the plate. In the off-season, the Cardinals asked for him back and we worked out another deal. We had helped them. They had sure as hell helped us. Now it was their turn again.

You could call that borderline hanky-panky, but it paid off like a lottery. That one little deal may have been the difference between going to the World Series and not going, which makes it a multi-million-dollar move.

I don't think I'm overstating. We *needed* that fourth-game win, because God knows if we'd had to face LaMarr Hoyt in the fifth game of the playoffs, it probably would have been the White Sox in the Series, not the Orioles. He was dominating that year.

Pitchers seem to have that one peak year—Hoyt that year, Stone in 1980, Ron Guidry when he was 25-3 in 1978, Orel Hershiser with his 23-8 in 1988, Bob Welch winning 27 in 1990. Guys like Sandy Koufax and Bob Gibson had more than one, but even Gibson had the one year (1968) with the 1.12 ERA. You hate to say it, but even as an opponent you have to admit it's a thing of beauty to watch a pitcher in a groove like that. You almost know you're going to get beat before you take the field. You're not going to tell anybody that, but you feel it inside.

I remember two years like that in particular: Hoyt's, and Denny McLain's in 1968, when he won 31 games.

McLain and Hoyt. Each of them wearing prison clothes when they should have still been in a baseball uniform.

I don't know how the hell two guys could be so smart when they walked across the white line to the pitcher's mound, and so dumb when they walked across the white line off the field.

11

Earl Weaver

Any time I'm asked to rate the great managers I have seen, I start with Walter Alston, and Whitey Herzog comes up very quickly. And I don't ever put together a list like that without including on it, way up high, the name of Earl Sidney Weaver.

He belongs. I know we gave Earl good ballplayers, some of them great players, but he did something with them. A manager can't take a lousy ballclub with poor talent, wave a magic wand and create hellish ballplayers, but a poor manager can mess up a good ballclub. And several have.

Earl had his quirks. They invented the Napoleonic Complex just for him. Whenever he went out on the mound, he always got on the very highest point of the mound, on the rubber. Always. And at 5-8, he still had to look up at a Jim Palmer (6-3).

Check Earl's rosters. He always had some guys around him he could look eye-to-eye. One year at our fall meetings, we were going through the list player by player when we got to Tom Shopay. He wasn't very good, but he was 5-9. Earl started lobbying for him (''You always need utility players...he gets on base... he does all the little things'') and kept escalating his pitch till I finally said, "Earl, for Christ's sake, you've got Shopay sounding like Clemente."

My relationship with Earl during the thirty years we were together could fill three books. There were some good times and some volatile times. We would argue till the wee hours of the morning, and those arguments would get hot. But they never became bitter, and that was because of the respect we had for each other. I know that was true from my end.

The first I heard Earl's name was in 1956 when my boss, Jim McLaughlin, the Orioles' farm director then, sent me to Knoxville, Tennessee, to watch the twenty-six-year-old kid who had just taken over as manager of the Sally League club there.

McLaughlin was sharp. He remembered Earl as a scrappy high school player at Beaumont High in St. Louis. McLaughlin was the Browns' farm director then, and both the Cardinals and the Browns were interested in Weaver. Earl picked the Cardinals, a decision that came up a time or two in our discussions, whenever Earl was getting too shot with his own intelligence. I told him one time, "You mean you could have signed with the Browns coming out of high school and you went for the Cardinals instead?"

He said, "Hell, yes."

"And you were a second baseman?"

"Yeah, a pretty damned good one."

"Earl, that just tells me how dumb you are. Jeezus Christ, didn't you read box scores? They had Red Schoendienst and you think a guy with your ability is going to make that club?"

He just laughed and said, "No, that wasn't it. I just wasn't good enough to play in the big leagues."

He's probably right, even for the Browns. Even in the minors, he never hit .300, although the little devil did drive in 101 runs one year when he had only two home runs. That's a pretty good trick in any league.

But he wasn't a major league player, period—which is something that came to mind for me immediately when Ken Harrelson moved from the radio broadcasting booth to take over the Chicago White Sox operation a few years ago and one of the first things he did was announce that he was getting rid of everybody in his system—managers or coaches—who hadn't been a major league player, on the grounds that today's young players wouldn't listen to anyone who hadn't been there. The three guys I just mentioned—Alston, Herzog and Weaver—will all be in the Hall of Fame and none of them took so much as a step toward Cooperstown with what they did as players. Harrelson lasted in that job less than a year, about as long as a guy with that kind of thinking figured to. There is no formula for what makes a good major league manager, but when one is found, it won't have much to do with the guy's own playing ability.

Earl had been up as high as Double-A but he was on his way back down at Single-A Knoxville when Dick Bartell, a pretty good major league shortstop in his day, was fired and Earl took over. Knoxville was an unaffiliated team, not part of anyone's farm system. McLaughlin asked me to stop by and see how he seemed to be doing.

I saw him in one game. Obviously, I didn't see anything special in just one game, but you could tell he hustled. And he made a couple of pitching changes, so he wasn't bashful about taking charge. I also sat down with him and asked a few questions, and I liked his answers. I told Jimmy, "I can't analyze the guy as a manager off one game. It looks like the guy is a bear-down type, but, hell—how can you go wrong? You must have thought something of him to even bring it up." He said, "I remember him as a guy who battled you and played hard even though his ability was limited." He hadn't ever been in their organization, but that shows what kind of job Jimmy McLaughlin did. He hired Earl and gave him his first shot in our organization—at Fitzgerald, Georgia, in the Georgia-Florida League, as far down as you can get. It was the beginning of a remarkable career.

Earl managed at every classification, from Class D all the way up through C, B, A, AA, AAA, including winter ball. He paid his dues, and he had outstanding records. He was in first place in more places than you can imagine. With some organizations, winning with minor league teams is no big thing. The theory is the emphasis is on developing individual players, not winning minor league games. True, development is the most important part, but the Orioles' idea that I always believed in was that you want players with winning attitudes, and you get that by playing on winners. It's not do-or-die in the minor leagues, but I wouldn't want my good kids playing for a losing team. Too many times kids who have done that come up to the big leagues and losing doesn't bother them all that much. I want every loss to hurt.

That's definitely the way Weaver operated in the minor leagues. I have a letter in my files dated July 29, 1961, when Earl was managing for us at Fox Cities in the Three-I League. It was from Vern Hoscheit, who was president of the league and a friend of mine. It was a cordial note which eventually got around:

"Your manager at Fox Cities has been a bit of a problem from the point of ejections. He has been tossed seven times. The last time I was in Fox Cities, we had a few Manhattans together and a big steak, and he's been trying very hard to stay in the ballpark since then. The guy is a real good manager and wants to win so bad he just loses his head on occasion."

He never changed.

Earl took to managing from the very first game. He had a feel for it. Let me draw a strange-sounding analogy with the basketball player I admired several years ago at Indiana and have ever since with the Detroit Pistons, Isiah Thomas. When Isiah brings the ball up, he can see the whole court, where most guys are capable of seeing only what's directly in front of them. That's Earl. He could visualize an entire ballgame and put each thing that happens in its proper perspective. He always had in the back of his mind what he would want to do in the seventh, eighth or ninth inning when he was playing the second inning. He also knew what he would do if the other guy did something—a counter move, or whatever. He just had that real good feel for it.

Two of his strengths stood out to me: he treated his players alike, and he never carried a grudge.

I honestly don't think his so-called stars got any more attention from Earl than his twenty-fifth guy, which I think is good in a manager. The guy who's playing every day—hell, he's happy.

It's the poor guy who seldom gets in there, who wants to play but is not good enough to be a regular—he's the guy Earl was smart enough to try to keep happy because you never know when circumstances are going to make you use him, maybe for a pretty long period.

Earl also asked the same things from his stars that he did from his fringe players. He had Reggie Jackson for only one season, but stars don't come any bigger than Reggie in his day and he wasn't too big for Earl to cut down.

I don't want to put Reggie in a bad light. Yes, he was the supreme hot dog, but I never saw the guy play any way but hard—real hard. That didn't put him above doing a little bit of testing off the field now and then.

We picked him up April 2, just in time to start the 1977 season, except he didn't report to us for a month. His first road trip with us was from Baltimore to Milwaukee on a charter. Our rule was always shirt, tie and coat at all times on the road. Reggie walked aboard the plane: no tie. He's got a coat and everything, but no tie.

Weaver already was in his seat, and we were ready to take off, but the minute he saw Reggie he jumped up. "No, no, Reggie, you can't get on *this* plane.

Reggie said, "What do you mean?"

"You know the rules. Everybody has a copy: coat and tie at all times on the road. You don't have a tie."

Reggie said he didn't have a tie.

"Then get off the plane."

Not many managers would have done that with a Reggie Jackson. Chuck Tanner wouldn't even have looked up.

Reggie walked off the plane with Dave Duncan, who had played with Reggie at Oakland but had been with us for a year. Jackson and Duncan had come to the airport together, and a few minutes after they left the plane, they came back and Reggie had a tie on.

Earl said to me, "Talk to him tomorrow. Tell him what our rules are."

The next morning I saw Reggie in the lobby of the Pfister

Hotel in Milwaukee. I said, "Reggie, the tie situation—that's not Earl's rule, that's a ballclub rule. We've had that rule for years, and Earl is just enforcing it." He said, "What the hell am I supposed to do when it's 98 degrees?" I said, "Wear a tie. You do the same thing that Palmer does, Brooks Robinson does—you wear a tie."

I looked at the tie he was wearing then, turned it around, and it said Gucci. Gucci ties even then were about fifty bucks apiece. I said, "Reggie, I'll bet you've got twenty-five of these." And he smiled. I said, "You were testing him, weren't you?" He said, "Yeah." I said, "You didn't get away with it, did you?" He said, "No."

Earl always had a pretty good grasp of how to get through to a player. As time went on, he grew to believe that fining a player, especially a big star, was the ultimate in futility, and I think he was right because salaries got to the place a fine would have to be damned near inconceivable to make a guy blink. Say Eddie Murray is making $2.4 million a year. You're going to bring him in line on something by saying, "I'm taking $500 of your money?"

The grudge thing I can testify to because even after our longest and most heated battles into the night, the next day started fresh for both of us. He managed the same way. He and Bobby Grich actually got into some pretty good shoving matches right on the bench, but it never changed anything with Earl. If he thought Grich could help him win a ballgame, his name was in the lineup and whatever happened between them, Earl would wipe out of his mind. To me, that's a hell of an attribute. I've heard managers say, "I'll show that son of a bitch. He won't play for seven days." That's stupid. That's ego showing, not discipline, and it's a good way to lose games—and jobs.

I thought Earl was particularly good at handling his pitching, which is very important. God knows you can mess up a pitching staff pretty well if you're not careful.

He communicated very closely with his pitching coach—George Bamberger, and later Ray Miller. Obviously the final decision is the manager's, but if Bamberger would say, "I think

so-and-so ought to miss a start. His arm might be a little tired,"
Earl would listen. It wouldn't have made any sense to have a
pitching coach he didn't have confidence in, but Earl was in
charge.

I felt Walter Alston did the same thing.

Earl's philosophy was a little different from Alston's. People
thought Earl was kind of a tricky guy. Alston did know all the
tricks, but Earl Weaver was one of the most conservative managers I ever saw—nothing tricky about him at all. He's so different from Herzog it's not even funny, when it comes to running
the ballgame. Whitey lives for the chance to steal a game with a
suicide squeeze in the eighth or ninth inning. Earl's philosophy
was to get as many guys on his club that had power as he could,
then sit back and enjoy three-run homers. I know that was his
reputation. I can tell you it was well earned. He was obsessed
with those three-run homers, but check our club out. We had
guys who could deliver them.

Earl's thinking was that, first of all, he didn't want to give up
an out. "You only get twenty-seven of them," he'd say. Besides, all that bunting and stuff just took the bat out of a hitter's
hands. He felt any time you gave a hitter a chance to swing, he
might hit one out.

Under Earl, we would put down a sacrifice bunt—
sometimes, but certainly not every time there was an opportunity. He would order a squeeze, but rarely. And we seldom
would hit-and-run. Billy Hunter was the third-base coach for
Earl for many years, and one of the best I've ever seen at that
job. The first year they worked together, Hunter said to me one
day, "I can't believe this, Jim. He doesn't even have a hit-and-
run sign." I said, "Billy, get used to it. He won't mess around
with a hit-and-run." Truthfully, there was another factor at work
there. Hunter always wanted the manager's job. He felt he
should have moved up from coach when Bauer was fired. Earl
was a coach on that 1968 team, too. It was my idea to make him
a coach, after he had managed twelve years and more than
1,500 games in the minor leagues. The reason I recommended
it was that I didn't think Bauer was getting the best that Boog

Powell had in him. And Powell and a lot of our other guys had played for Weaver in the minors.

Still, what Hunter said was absolutely true. Rich Dauer was the one player on our club with a hit-and-run sign. *His* sign. When he wanted to put it on, he'd give it to Earl. And Rich knew that he damned well better make it work, if he put it on.

So, OK, what I'm saying about Earl's game managing is that it was pretty basic. His biggest plus was that he knew what he could get out of a player, and he was damned good at getting it all out. Check Boog Powell's stats the year before Weaver came up (.234, 13 homers, 55 RBIs) and the first full year he managed (.304, 37 homers, 121 RBIs).

Psychologically he was pretty shrewd, too. For example: Jim Palmer had a lot of physical problems. Even though he had a nice, fluid motion that looked like it didn't put a strain on anything, he wound up with problems in his arm, his shoulder and his back, at different times. Earl knew Palmer's makeup as well as he knew his son's. So, let's say Palmer has been unable to pitch for a week, but now he's starting to come back and today he's throwing a little on the sideline prior to a ballgame. Earl never would sit in his office and tell his pitching coach, "Let me know how he looks, George." No, no. Not Earl. He would go right out there himself, to make it absolutely plain to Palmer without saying a word that " I am interested in you. That's why I'm here, to see whether or not you are ready. You're a vital man, in my eyes." Palmer, or anybody else, had to like that.

Those two had a pretty good thing going for years, too. They were two strong-willed competitors who did have their differences. Weaver would get very upset when he thought Palmer was throwing well but Jim would ask to be taken out. And there were times when it worked the other way, too—Jim thought he still had good stuff and Earl pulled him. They would go around and around, taking shots at each other. I used to laugh when writers or just plain fans would say to me, "Boy, they must hate each other. Did you see what Palmer said about Weaver (or Weaver about Palmer, or both) in the newspaper this morning?" Forget it. It was their own long-running game. They were needling each other, and whoever got the last shot in won that confrontation. Five days later, the other guy might win one, but each of them had a hell of a lot of respect for the other.

It was hard for Earl to believe writers or anybody else could think he had anything but the greatest feeling for Palmer. During one of those times late in Palmer's career when they were supposed to be feuding, Earl was looking at Jim's lifetime stats. He said to me, "Look at this. How in the hell can I *not* like the man? Look at the complete games. Look at the innings pitched. I don't like a guy who's given me that kind of effort?"

Earl knew Palmer gave him the best that he had to give. And I think Jim knew that maybe nobody else would have gotten all of that out of him.

Earl could be almost overly loyal to his players. If a guy had done a hell of a job for him, Earl found it very hard to forget. He'd go as long with that guy as he possibly could before giving up on him. That backfires sometimes, but overall it's an attribute.

The first change Weaver made on the day he replaced Hank Bauer as manager of the Orioles was to put Don Buford in the lineup, every day. Buford was a former Southern Cal football player, competitive as hell. Bauer would put him in one day, hold him out the next—play him in the infield one day, the outfield maybe the next. Earl put him in the outfield and kept him there, every day. Buford responded and played well. He had good years. He played hard. He helped us win a lot of games.

But in 1972, he had slowed down and regressed as a player. He was just really struggling, but with Earl there was always that tug of loyalty: "The guy did it for me. He helped me win. I just can't..." So, his name would be in the lineup again; 0-for-4. Then the next day, "Yeah, but..."

In the meantime, we've got a situation at second base with Bobby Grich at twenty-three, trying to get established in the big leagues a year later than he probably should have, and Davey Johnson at twenty-nine still pretty good. Earl is trying to keep them both happy, playing Johnson one day and Grich the next.

Hey, we're talking about two pretty good ballplayers, and we're pissing both of them off.

One night in a bar, at about 2 A.M.—I don't even know what town we were in but it was in August and we still had a shot at winning if we could just find some offense—I said, "Earl, I want you to think about something. Buford is struggling. He's reached the stage in his career when he's going backward." He said, "Yeah, he is." I said, "You're trying to keep Grich and Johnson happy at the same time and you can't do it because they both want to play. Why don't you sit Buford down and put Grich in left field for the rest of the season? He's a hell of an athlete. He'll adjust. And then you've got both of them in the lineup every day."

He said, "That's a great idea."

He never did it.

I was a little green myself then, because it upset me. I sat down with Frank Cashen a few weeks later and said, "Dammit, Frank, I'm really upset. The ballclub should be better than it's playing. Buford is having a real rough time. I think he's had it." And I told him about the Grich move I had suggested. Wise old Frank said: "Russo, you made one mistake. You should have made it sound like it was his idea, not yours."

So charge me with that one. If I hadn't made that mistake, I think we'd have had a chance to win that year, too.

The further Earl went into his managing career, the smarter he got about dealing with umpires. He never got truly good, but he had some valid complaints on that score, too. The umpires didn't always deal with him as they should have.

The worst example involved Ron Luciano, the former Syracuse football lineman who did some umpiring and wrote some books about it and, in my opinion, was a hell of a lot better writer than umpire. And I didn't like his writing at all.

In 1975 we started hearing that Luciano, building a reputation as a "funny" after-dinner speaker, was using the line: "I don't care who wins, as long as it's not the Baltimore Orioles or

Earl Weaver." In 1976, he told a *Chicago Sun-Times* columnist: "I don't care who wins as long as it's not Baltimore, and I hope Weaver loses every game."

The column was the breaking point, as far as the Orioles were concerned. How in the hell can a league put a man like that in the role of neutral arbitrator? It happened that 1976 was the year Indiana won the NCAA basketball championship with an unbeaten team—a great team with a great coach that I think the world of, Bob Knight. As I read that Luciano quote, I tried to draw analogies. How long would the Big Ten keep a referee who said publicly, "I don't care who wins as long as it's not Indiana or Bob Knight?" What would the NFL do, or the NBA? Or even tennis, if one of those imperious guys in a highchair said something like that about Jimmy Connors?

We protested immediately, to the league office. Weaver and Frank Cashen made their feelings known very clearly to the league president, Lee MacPhail. I don't think that should have been necessary. To me, MacPhail was gutless for not stepping in on his own, after a comment like that, and firing Luciano. Immediately. Instead, Earl said, "I don't want that guy umpiring any of our games any more." The answer they heard was, "OK." Luciano didn't work any Orioles games the rest of that season, and not many the following seasons.

He worked on Bill Haller's crew, and Dale Ford replaced him. The crew carried along without him, in Weaver-bashing. If statistics were available, I'm sure they would show that Bill Haller ran Weaver more often than any other umpire. For example: rules forbid smoking in the dugout, but managers forever and ever have sneaked an anxious puff or two at times—right to this day with one of the very best: Jim Leyland of the Pirates. Haller would throw Weaver out for that.

But we didn't see much of Luciano till an incident in Chicago August 26, 1979. In the fifth inning, Doug DeCinces was batting for us, and a 3-and-2 pitch came in a good foot outside. DeCinces threw his bat away and was halfway to first base when Luciano yelled, "Strike three."

Naturally DeCinces argued. Naturally Weaver ran out to intervene and keep his player in the game. DeCinces surprised Weaver by abruptly leaving the debate, which left Weaver and Luciano staring at each other. And naturally Luciano threw him out.

The next step came naturally, too. Weaver told the P.A. announcer: "I want it announced that I am protesting this game, because of an umpire's integrity."

I feel now, and I told him then, he had every right to do exactly what he did, except he used the wrong word. "Integrity" might have been a bit strong. I don't see how anyone could have argued if he had said "because of an umpire's prejudice." What the hell else is it when a guy is openly rooting against you? Maybe Earl was right—Luciano's integrity was the issue.

Naturally, (1) the protest didn't work, (2) Earl was fined by the league office, and (3) Earl was suspended. Pause a minute to put that situation up against the one in 1991 when Reds manager Lou Piniella, still simmering a day after a blown home run call, publicly accused the offending umpire, Gary Darling, of bias. Going back to numbers: (1) Lou was out of bounds; that charge—especially after a day to think about it—was too much; (2) considering the precedent of the MacPhail action, could you blame Weaver if he was a bit shocked when National League President Bill White took no action at all to discipline Piniella? and (3) the situation produced the grandstand play of the year: Darling and the umpires' union suing Piniella for $5 million for defamation of character. One question: where the hell was the umpires' union when Luciano was so proud of his bias he made it into a stand-up comedy line? What a joke—Luciano as an umpire *and* the lawsuit.

Weaver was not easily subdued. During his suspension, he and I were sitting in the stands at Minnesota watching our club, and all of sudden he said, "Tug your cap."

I'm giving signs to Frank Robinson.

Umpire Nestor Chylak happened to be sitting up there, recovering from the heart attack that had sidelined him, and he said, "Jee-zus, Earl, you can't do THAT."

We didn't stop but I tried to be a little less obvious. Nestor was a good guy, and a great umpire.

Besides, I always had the feeling Earl valued my scouting more than he did my "help" in managing. He listened in totally different ways, and I can't honestly say that he ever second-guessed my scouting recommendations.

Before the 1979 World Series with Pittsburgh, Alan Goldstein wrote in the *Baltimore Sun*:

"When E.F. Hutton talks, everybody listens. And when Jim Russo talks, Earl Weaver listens.

"Russo, the Orioles' superscout who has been tracking the Pittsburgh Pirates the last two weeks on their march to the National League pennant, yesterday whispered one word in Weaver's ear: 'Flanagan.'"

OK, that *was* the relationship. Earl did listen.

What he heard me say was the strength of that Pirates team was its left-handed hitters—not just Willie Stargell and Dave Parker as the obvious leaders, but also John Milner, who concerned me more than Bill Robinson, the right-handed hitter they used against lefties. . .and Omar Moreno, who I felt we *had* to keep off base because his speed got everything going for the power guys behind him. In my thirty-five years of scouting, the fastest I ever caught a man going from home to first base was 3.3 seconds, and it was Omar Moreno—on a push bunt to shortstop, batting left-handed.

So, yes, I did say we should open the series with a left-hander, but the truth was I suggested Scott McGregor rather than Flanagan.

Earl said, "Russo, you can tell me I should pitch a left-hander, and I'll do it. But, God dammit, I'll decide which left-hander."

That was Earl, and there wasn't an ounce of one-upmanship in it. Maybe a half-ounce of stubbornness.

He didn't make a bad choice. Flanagan won 23 games for us that year and won the Cy Young Award. And he won the opener, 5-4. My man McGregor came along in the third game and won it, 8-4, so we're both looking good. In fact, we're up 3-1 and

Flanagan goes for the clincher—and pitches pretty well, but he's down 2-1 in the seventh and Earl has to hit for him. Our bullpen fails and we lose 7-1.

It was the start of one of the most amazing things I've ever seen in baseball. From the time Earl pinch hit for Flanagan—a move that was absolutely correct in any baseball "book"—until the end of the Series, every move that Weaver made turned out wrong and every one that Chuck Tanner made for the Pirates came out right. I love Chuck Tanner as a person, but he isn't close to Weaver as a manager or tactician or anything else, not remotely close. But damned if Tanner doesn't steer the Pirates from the 3-1 deficit to win, only the fourth time in World Series history a team did that, and he won the seventh game when my man McGregor got a ball down to Stargell, where you don't want to put it on most left-handed power hitters and you sure didn't want to with that one.

The book I had on Stargell said, "Start him belt-high and keep climbing with the fastball." Willie, winding down his career with a year that clinched him entrance into the Hall of Fame, jumped on that low pitch for a two-run homer in the sixth inning of Game 7. We went from up 1-0 to down 2-1 and lost 4-1. And I'll swear we lost that game and Series doing everything right. As John F. Kennedy said, "Who said life is fair?" Spoken like the true Red Sox fan he was.

Sometimes Weaver's bullheadedness got him beaten fairly and squarely. Earl managed the American League in the 1970 All-Star Game in Cincinnati. The night before the game, he and I were sitting in the bar at the Netherlands Hilton, American League headquarters for the game. Hell, it must have been three in the morning, and it was my fault we were still going because I couldn't hold myself back from challenging him on what I thought was a bad mistake: the pitching staff he had selected for the game.

I asked him: "Earl, why the hell didn't you pick a couple of relief pitchers? We're going to go into that damned ballgame tomorrow with our hands tied behind our backs—no relief pitcher."

He said, "What the hell do you mean? I don't need a relief pitcher."

He picked all starters. We've got Jim Palmer, Catfish Hunter, Sam McDowell, Jim Perry, Mike Cuellar, Dave McNally, Clyde Wright, Fritz Peterson, Mel Stottlemyre—I don't even have to look at the book to remember, because the names rattled through my mind so much from the day Earl sat down with American League president Lee MacPhail, our old boss, and made up the pitching list without Sparky Lyle, Ron Perranoski, Lindy McDaniel, or any one of a dozen relief pitchers who were having pretty good years. Hell, I blame Lee for part of that. He knew Earl. He knew he had to put his foot down, because nobody wanted to break that unbelievable losing streak we had in All-Star games more than Lee MacPhail did. But he let Earl have his way.

I'm not built to just go along. That night at the Netherlands Hilton, I've got to unload. "Dammit, Earl, you're ignoring a specialty. You're telling all the relievers in our league, 'I don't need you. Your specialty doesn't mean a damned thing to me.' You *had* to pick Sparky Lyle and at least three relievers."

He said, "You're trying to tell me that Clyde Wright can't come in and do as good a job as Sparky Lyle?"

"Absolutely. That's exactly what I'm trying to tell you. Lyle does it all year long. You use relief pitchers during the season. What the hell is the difference, just because it's an All-Star game?"

He said, "As long as I manage an All-Star team, there will not be any relief pitchers."

We went around and around on that theme and always ended up in the same positions. Finally at 3 A.M. I said, "Aw, go to hell, Earl. I'm going to bed."

So...

You remember the game for the way Pete Rose ran over Ray Fosse to score the winning run. Hell, that one play is so frozen in everybody's mind that I would bet the average fan would say the score of the game was 1-0.

I can damned well tell you it wasn't 1-0, and Rose should

never have had the chance to win the game. We led 4-1 going into the ninth inning. Palmer had pitched his three innings nicely. McDowell had pitched his three. Perry had pitched two. And here came Earl with Catfish to wrap it up in the ninth and stick it to all the Jim Russo's of the world who had dared to second-guess the master.

The problem with a Catfish Hunter or almost any other great pitcher—Cuellar was a classic example—was that if you were ever going to get him, it was probably in the first inning. When he was settled into his own great groove, he would paint the corners of the plate like a master and pitch—just plain pitch. Lord, he could pitch.

But I sat there in the stands at Riverfront Stadium and burned, because Catfish got one guy out, and then Dick Dietz homered and Bud Harrelson singled and Joe Morgan singled— and here we are with Willie McCovey at the plate as the go-ahead run. It's the perfect time to bring in Sparky Lyle, who's used to just that kind of situation, but we don't have him for left-handed relief, we've got Fritz Peterson. McCovey rips a single off him, and it's 4-3 with the tying run on third and Roberto Clemente up. Gotta have a double play or strikeout; perfect time for a Lindy McDaniel. But we've got Stottlemyre, and Clemente drives a deep fly ball that finishes the job of blowing our lead.

The Rose play happened in the twelfth, an hour after we should have been celebrating.

Two days later, Lee MacPhail made a statement out of the American League office in New York: "Henceforth, there will be relief pitchers on the American League All-Star staff." Great. I won the argument and lost the damned game.

12

In Company with Earl

Other managers who impressed me, in addition to Earl Weaver? There's only a handful that I thought were outstanding. I was always hard to please.

Walter Alston bordered on greatness, in my estimation. Some of his former players might not agree with me. One of them was Pee Wee Reese, one of the nicest people in the world but no Walter Alston fan. I think even Pee Wee would say, though, that the Alston he played for, breaking into managing, was different from the manager he became ten, fifteen, twenty years on the job.

I just thought Walter's teams did the thing I always like to see when I watch a baseball, basketball or football team: mistake-free play. Their execution day after day after day was just outstanding. So few mistakes. It was just a thrill to watch them play and execute, and I think that's a reflection on the manager, the way he prepares them. Even with good players, the execution isn't always going to be there the way it was with the Dodgers when Alston had them. I just felt he was a hell of a manager.

Some of it, too, was the Dodger organization. I wouldn't

want to grade Tommy Lasorda down as a manager—he's a good manager, very skilled in handling players, with a long record of success to prove it. But there's something wrong now in that system. I don't know if they're not getting the point across in the minor leagues, but when I see them play now I see mistake after mistake. It isn't all the manager. Fundamental baseball has to start in the minor leagues.

Whitey Herzog unquestionably is one of the best managers. More than anyone I've ever watched, he can adapt his style of managing to the type ballclub he has. He's not one of these staid, headstrong guys—"I don't care if I do have a lot of power on this ballclub, I'm going to still have them bunting and running." If he had a lot of power, he used it. If he didn't, he adapted. He belongs in the upper echelon.

I liked Tony LaRussa before he won a division title with the White Sox, let alone the World Series with the A's.

Bill Veeck gave Tony his first managing job, and in those days, Veeck's managers had one final duty after every night game: come to the Bards' Room (the press bar upstairs at Comiskey Park) after everything else was done and have a chat and maybe a beer or two with the boss. I was there for some of those, and I remember one time Tony said to me:

"Tommy John is going to pitch against us tomorrow. I've been thinking about starting four left-handed hitters against him. What do you think?"

John was left-handed, of course, but Tony's point was that John had spent his whole career making right-handed hitters beat his sinker into the ground—and left-handed hitters usually are better low ball hitters.

I said, "Hell, that sounds like a good idea to me, Tony. It's sure as hell worth trying. Give it a shot."

He started four left-handed hitters against John the next night, and Tommy got eighteen groundball outs.

The idea was there but the result was the same. But it showed me LaRussa was a young guy with a live mind who wasn't fenced in by convention—or afraid to be the guy who dared to go against one of the best left-handers in the game with a lineup intentionally stocked with left-handed hitters. It didn't work, but a lot of things Tony has done since then—against the book and with it—sure have.

Sparky Anderson is a good manager—just excellent as far as running the ballgame is concerned.

I don't always feel his abilities to judge a ballplayer are as good as maybe some of the others. Sparky has tendencies to get carried away a little bit. One year, he was ready to move the best second baseman in the American League, Lou Whitaker, to third base because he had a rookie named Chris Pitino he raved about. It turned out the kid couldn't play. Whitaker was just great during all that, a true pro. All he said publicly was, "I don't mind moving over—anything to help the club." Can you imagine that? In *this* era? But after a little while, Lou got a chance to take a look at this guy, and he very quietly let Sparky know, "I don't think I want to leave second base." He didn't, and he went on after that to have the best years of his life.

That doesn't lessen Sparky's abilities as far as running a ballgame or a ballclub. It's just that he broke in as a big league manager surrounded by some of the greatest players of the era on that Big Red Machine at Cincinnati and he sometimes gives me the impression he thinks he's going to see a Johnny Bench or a Joe Morgan or a Pete Rose sprout in front of his eyes every spring or so. They've been voting people into Cooperstown for more than fifty years now but I'm not sure which would be the bigger number: guys who are in there now or the ones who played for Sparky that he made sound like Hall of Famers.

That makes it a little funny that one time he and I disagreed in the opposite direction on one of his players, who I apparently thought was better than Sparky did.

I was still working for the Orioles in 1984 when the *New York Times* called me just prior to the World Series with an idea for a story: I would do a scout's review of the Tigers and Dave

Johnson, managing the Mets then, would do one on the Padres. I was pleased with the way my part of it came out—hell, they paid me $1,500 for a couple of hours of work. I was beginning to think I had underestimated sportswriting as a line of work till I talked afterward to a couple of writers and found out that wasn't quite scale.

The thrust of my report was that the Tigers were awfully good, which they proved by winning in five games. I did comment that sometimes sort of a fringe player comes out in the World Series and becomes the MVP, and the sleeper-type guy I mentioned as a possibility to do that was Howard Johnson.

Bill Lajoie, the Tigers' general manager then, told me later that he and Jim Campbell, club president at the time and later chairman of the board, were talking with Sparky just prior to the World Series. One of them said, "What do you think about playing Howard Johnson every day at third base in this Series?" Sparky said, "I don't have that in mind at all." Lajoie said he mentioned, "Jim Russo thinks he may have an outside shot at being MVP in the World Series." And Sparky said, "He's still not gonna play."

And he didn't. Sparky won the Series with Marty Castillo playing third base and hitting .333, so you sure can't say he made a mistake. But the way Howard Johnson has played for the Mets ever since the Tigers traded him over there says I wasn't too far off, either. I felt then and I think it's obvious now that Howard can get hot for a few days, and he's got some pop in his bat. You make a mistake and he can hurt you.

But Sparky's all right, definitely one of the better ones.

Gene Mauch isn't in my first six because I think he had too many chances to win and blew them. The man never made the World Series. I remember some researcher from *Sports Illustrated* called me one day and said, "We're doing a story on Gene Mauch and it will be called 'Gene Mauch, the Genius.' You've seen him manage a while. What can you say?" I said, "Nothing. You've called the wrong man. I don't think he is a genius." I didn't care much for the premise of that story.

I can't pull harder for a guy to make it as a manager than I do for Frank Robinson. It's hard for Frank to understand why his players can't execute like he did. It pained me when the Orioles fired him less than a fourth of the way into the 1991 season, but firing is the unfortunate part of a manager's way of life.

I really like what I've seen from Jim Leyland, with the Pirates. He was impressive in leading the Pirates to the division championship in 1990, but I thought he made a big step toward the top level in spring training the next year. The National League MVP was Barry Bonds, but right there in the spring—with cameras going and the whole world watching—Leyland let Bonds know, and through him everybody else on the ballclub, that the manager was running the club. Period. God, I loved to see that. And Bonds helped Leyland and the Pirates repeat in 1991.

Even before that spring training incident, Leyland was respected throughout baseball. In my judgment, he's one of the best young managers in the game. I'm convinced he's going to be around a long time and win a lot. He's got what it takes.

I thought at one time Dave Bristol was going to be a hell of a manager. Then it just seems to me that Dave kinda turned into a politician. At times he would be so rigid that the ballplayers just turned against him. You can't do it. I don't believe in babying them, but you've got to be flexible. This is the thing I told Cal Ripken, Sr., when he became our manager: "Cal, this is not D, C or B any more. You say something to those kids down there and they're going to do it. At this level, you're going to have to exercise caution because if you're too rigid you'll lose them, and if you baby the hell out of them, you've lost them, too."

It's a fine point. You've got to be awful careful to balance the thing. You can be buddy-buddy, pat them on the back and they'll say, "We've got this son of a bitch right were we want him." Players will take advantage of you.

Lou Piniella emerged as a hot young genius when the Reds swept the favored A's in the 1990 World Series. And he did impress me as a good manager, a real fine manager, because he won the National League playoffs and the Series by knowing his club's strengths and using them well.

Lou was a minor league outfielder in our organization for a couple of years, and his concept of baseball then started and ended with a bat. He was a hell of a competitor—too much of one, for his and his team's good. He'd fly out, and he'd storm back to the dugout so mad he'd smash a batting helmet and kick the water cooler.

I remember talking to him like a father after one of those outbursts: "You seem to think you've got to go 4-for-4 every day. I've got news for you. You're not going to bat 1.000." It seemed logical enough to me, but while we had him he never did understand that.

Later on, he made the big leagues and became a good hitter. He was with Kansas City in 1972 when Earl Weaver told him he was putting him on the All-Star team. "And, by the way, Lou," Weaver told him, "you can leave your glove at home."

It wasn't a very subtle way of saying he was going to get one pinch-hitting chance, at best—and there was no way he would be allowed to play defense. And that's what happened: he pinch-hit, grounded out, and his All-Star career record is 0-for-1.

As the Reds' manager in the fall of 1990, though, Piniella was anything but a free-swinger. He played to get a run early, to try to get to his bullpen with any kind of lead. It was exactly the right way for him to manage, because his pitching staff was perfect for that—good but not exceptional starters, good middle relief, and two exceptional closers, right-handed or left-handed.

It was a textbook case of managing according to the type of ballclub he had. He started that the first day of spring training. He had a team that had been picked to win its division year after year and found a way to lose every time. He let them know right away that they were a team good enough to win and they were cheating themselves if they didn't exert enough effort and play with enough desire and intelligence to capitalize on the ability they had. All year long he made his team believe it could win. And darned if it didn't. That's good managing.

I thought the man Piniella replaced at Cincinnati, Pete Rose, had a chance to be a pretty good manager, until all of his troubles came up and made his job impossible. The game moves I saw him make I liked but unfortunately that became a minor part of what was going on for him and the Reds before he finally went on suspension in 1989. That's a sad story. I don't think he was overpunished, but I also don't think he'll ever be back in the game that has been everything to him. The main question left for him is whether his gambling and tax problems should take him out of consideration for the Hall of Fame. I don't get a vote there. If I did, Pete Rose the player certainly would be on my Hall of Fame ballot. Hell, only two guys in the history of the game had 4,000 hits, and the other guy got in as a charter member with more votes than Babe Ruth. And from what I've heard, if they come up with a way to calculate morality points for both of those 4,000-hit guys, Pete Rose may come out ahead of Ty Cobb.

But if Pete did bet on baseball, he should not be allowed in Cooperstown. That's crossing a line that simply can't be crossed.

I do think Pete would have been better equipped to manage if he had spent some time running a club in the minor leagues. Today's players seem to think that's beneath them, but I think it's invaluable. It's awfully tough for a guy to come right off the field as a player, where his primary concern was getting himself ready to play every day, and start coping with twenty-five different personalities.

That brings up one of the real enigmas in this task of rating managers: the late Billy Martin. So many pluses. So many minuses. But what a tragic waste.

The day I heard Billy had died in an auto accident, I felt a hundred memories crashing into each other in my brain...
"George is a murderer"...Gonzalo Marquez...Denver...
Floyd Bannister.

At the end of Billy's playing days, when he was a part-time player with the Reds, he got into a fight—hard as that is to imagine—with a Cub pitcher named Jim Brewer. It wasn't a typical baseball fight. Billy got in a shot that broke Brewer's jaw, and Brewer sued. So, in 1962, when Billy was through as a player and coaching for the Minnesota Twins, there was a warrant out against him in Chicago. When the Twins went in to play the White Sox, the Minnesota ballclub suggested that Billy just go to Cincinnati for a few days and take a look at some National League ballgames, then rejoin the club after the Chicago stop.

I was in Cincinnati then, too, and Billy told me, "I don't see how they can get along without me, Jim. Those players want me there. For three days I won't be there." I thought, Jesus Christ. This stuff is getting kinda thick.

But in our conversation he mentioned how much he wanted to manage in the big leagues some day, and he said the managing job with the Twins' Triple-A team at Denver had just opened and the club had offered him the job. He wasn't inclined to go. He told me, "I think I'm more valuable to them coaching third base. I don't think there's anybody there who can coach third base like I can coach it."

I just looked him in the eye and said, "You say you want to manage in the big leagues? Go to Denver. They've done you a hell of a favor, Billy. There are twenty-one ballplayers on a Triple-A roster. You'll have a chance to cope with twenty-one different personalities—this guy might need a little encouragement, and this guy might need a kick in the ass. That's what you'll have to do in the big leagues. Go manage. It will help you much more than to stay in there the rest of the season as a coach."

He did go, and then he got his break and took full advantage of it.

He was probably as successful a quick-fix type manager as the game has seen, but it didn't take long for him to start wearing real thin. About all anyone remembers about him now is that carnival parade of five times in and five times out under George Steinbrenner with the Yankees, and then Billy had a reputation as the tough guy brought in to make an underachieving Yankee team buckle down and play hard. Before he got into all of that, though, he managed the Twins, the Tigers and the A's, and achieved quick-fixes at each of those spots. Billy would be like a breath of fresh air, initially. He would be tough, he would win, the air would turn sour, and he would leave.

He had an astoundingly irritating way of letting you know, all the time, that he was his own man. For example . . .

In 1972, he won the AL East championship with Detroit, and he was getting ready to play Oakland in the playoffs. Detroit had two scouts following Oakland, just as I had because we had been in the race. One day, just out of the clear blue sky, Billy asked me, "What can you tell me about Oakland?"

There aren't any written rules in scouting, but I don't think it's exactly professional to be in a position to upstage the Detroit guys who were writing their own report for Billy, so I just said, "You've got two guys to listen to, Billy." But he kept coming: "What can *you* tell me?"

I said, "Billy, I'm not going to tell you anything about Oakland, except one thing: Don't let Gonzalo Marquez beat you with a fastball. That son of a bitch can hit the fastball."

Marquez was a fringe area player with the A's, almost strictly a pinch-hitter. I just had to come up with something to get him off my back, and I thought Gonzalo Marquez was about as minimal as I could be in crossing professional lines. He said, "Thanks, Jim. I'll remember that."

So, the playoffs open in Oakland, and in the very first game, the Tigers take a 2-1 lead in the top of the eleventh, and in the bottom of the inning, the A's put the tying run on second and up comes Gonzalo Marquez to pinch hit.

I'm sitting there watching and fastball, fastball, fastball. Seven in a row. He fouled them off till finally he drove one up the middle to tie the game, and the A's go on to win it that inning. And in my mind, Billy went down that day determined to show Jim Russo wherever he was that he didn't know as much about baseball as he damned well thought he did.

But don't get me wrong, I thought he was a hell of a guy,

fun to be with. There were times I'd rather not have been around him, but there were times when I didn't really want to be around Weaver, either. And, as was the case with Earl and me, Billy and I didn't always agree—like one night in Seattle...

The Orioles had a rule that a player could not drink at the bar at the hotel where the club is staying. Some clubs have it and some don't, but I think it's a great rule. You avoid the situation where you've played a game, a player who has had some drinks sees the manager across the room and says, ''That son of a bitch. He's not handling me right.'' And here you go.

Billy apparently didn't have that rule. His ballplayers would frequent the same bar Billy did. A lot of incidents that checkered Billy's career would have been avoided with that one simple rule.

It wouldn't have applied to me, anyway, and whenever I'd cover one of Billy's ballclubs, he'd usually say, ''Let's get together at the hotel bar.'' This gave us a chance to talk. And that's what happened one night in Seattle, when he was with the Yankees and his club had just been handled pretty well by Floyd Bannister, who was with the Mariners then.

Billy said, ''What did you think of Bannister?'' I said, ''Good stuff. He looked real, real good.''

He said, ''Real good? If he's not the best left-hander in baseball I don't know what the hell I'm doing.''

I thought, ''Wait a minute, I like the guy but the best left-hander in baseball?'' It was 1979, and names like Steve Carlton, John Candelaria, Jerry Koosman, our Scotty McGregor and Mike Flanagan, hell, even Ron Guidry on Billy's club, ran through my mind and I said, ''I'm not going to go that far.''

Art Fowler, his pitching coach and drinking buddy, was with him and he said, ''I don't know, Jim, I've never seen anything like that.''

I said, ''We've got a couple of guys by the name of Flanagan and McGregor. They're not exactly a couple of potted plants.''

It pissed Martin off. He got up and as he and Fowler were leaving, he said, ''You don't think I know anything about pitching, do you?'' I thought, "Truthfully, no.'' But I decided I had been honest enough already and let it pass.

He did raise a point of vulnerability, though, in evaluating him as a manager. In 1980, his first year at Oakland, he came up with a remarkable group of young pitchers—Rick Langford, Mike Norris, Steve McCatty and Matt Keough. The A's had lost 108 games the year before, but under Billy they jumped to 83-79 the next year, a 29-game improvement, and finished second. He was everybody's Manager of the Year, but in getting there he extracted 290 innings and 28 complete games from Langford (28 years old), 284 innings and 24 complete games from Norris (25), 250 innings and 20 complete games from Keough (25) and 222 innings and 11 complete games from McCatty (26). That's not necessarily too many games or innings for a healthy arm, but someone had better be keeping a pretty close count on pitches and that wasn't something Billy paid any attention to. Norris in particular had some games with a lot of pitches.

Two years later, all but Keough spent some time on the disabled list with arm problems, and three years later, the four who had gone 71-48 for Billy in 1980 were a combined 15-25. No, Billy, I'd have to say I didn't think pitching was one of your long suits.

Once he and Steinbrenner found each other, bizarre things were inevitable. I knew that, and expected that. Most of the time, Billy would rave about what a great guy George Steinbrenner is, and I think they truly did like each other very much. But Billy would get a drink or two in him and grumble to me: "If it wasn't for me, this ballclub would be in last place.'' Or, "He won't get me any help.'' Stuff like that. But still I wasn't prepared for the night Billy and I were sitting across a table in a bar and he blurted out, "George is a murderer.''

I said, "What are you talking about?''

This was three years after the shocking mid-season plane crash that killed Yankee catcher Thurman Munson, but that's what was on Billy's mind. His reasoning: "George shouldn't have given him permission to fly the plane. He'd be alive today if George didn't do that. He's a murderer, that's what he is.''

That's reaching deep, but that was Billy. As a manager, he was a good strategist, but his tactics weren't as good as he thought. I can't put Billy in my top category. There were just too many involvements that eliminate him from being in that group. I liked to watch a manager when his club was losing—did he panic, or did he manage? If you can't control yourself, how can you control twenty-five players? Billy was such a tense person that little things that should remain minute erupted into big, important things. When you manage in the big leagues or anyplace else, making the lineup and giving signs aren't your only responsibilities. I just don't think Billy met the extra criteria.

I would put the guy who was Billy's working model as a manager on my list—high. Casey Stengel ran a real good ship— when he had a good ship, with the great Yankee teams of the 1950s. And he ran a pretty good ship when he had a very bad one, with the original Mets.

Modern ideas about platooning probably emanated from Casey more than any other manager, and the funny part was that Casey hit upon it as a way out of a dilemma nobody else had: too much talent. He'd have a Gene Woodling and Johnny Lindell available for one spot, or Hank Bauer and Irv Noren, or Bobby Brown and Gil McDougald, or Elston Howard to plug in for Yogi Berra or Norm Siebern, lefty-righty combinations all over the place. Managers do it now with average players. Casey did it to keep guys happy who would have been starting anyplace else.

Then, when fate showed him its flipside with the pathetic early Mets, I thought he handled that great, too. He injected just enough humor that you had to say to yourself, ''I don't think this is getting him down.'' For a guy going from one of the best ballclubs ever to one of the worst teams ever, I thought he was philosophical. As good as Earl was, I don't think he could have done that. The losing would have just killed him.

That Stengel situation illustrates something: a great manager in one situation might not be right at all for another one. I read once where Branch Rickey said if he had a team that could win the pennant, there was no manager he'd rather have than Leo Durocher—and if he had one that had no chance at all, there was no manager he'd rather *not* have than Durocher.

I liked Durocher. I thought he was a classy individual, and one of the best managers I saw. The day he died, I—and I think most people who knew him, in baseball or out—felt an ache for the void in his life that was never filled: election to the Hall of Fame. Without any question, I think he deserves to be there.

But I wouldn't have wanted him in the situation Casey had, with an expansion team. Some of the best managers that I've seen in baseball I would not want managing an expansion club, because it takes a man of great patience. Earl Weaver? Billy Martin? No way. They were too accustomed to winning.

But a Chuck Tanner? He didn't have enough discipline for me, if he were to be given a team that could win it—even though he beat us in the 1979 World Series with a pretty talented club. I like the guy—a genuinely good person. But what always comes into my mind when I think of Chuck Tanner is his handling of Richie Allen with the White Sox. He probably got the best anyone could have pulled out of Allen in his MVP year (1972), and Allen at his best was good enough to make the White Sox a contender when no one expected it—and to revive the whole franchise when it was about to die.

But there was a cost. Tanner let Allen do anything he wanted to do—and had the audacity to tell his club what he was doing: "We're going to have to overlook a lot of things he does, fellas. He's got a chance to put a lot of money in our pockets." I couldn't believe that. In other words, "I'm the manager, fellas, and there's going to be one set of rules for you and one set for Richie." Richie would get to the ballpark sometimes just in time to put the damned uniform on and go out and stand up for the national anthem. The others had to be there two and a half hours before game time. Team rules didn't apply to him, only to the other twenty-four.

And it carried over. In 1974, the fans voted Allen to the All-Star Game. He got to the Pittsburgh ballpark twenty-five minutes before the game was ready to start, and I'll be damned if

Dick Williams, the manager, didn't let him start. The All-Star Game! I'd have said, "I don't give a damn how many votes you got, you're not starting this ballgame."

That winter at the convention, I was sitting with Chuck and his wife, Rebecca. "Jim," he said, "Richie Allen could help you guys. He's a pretty damned good ballplayer."

I said, "Chuck, you don't have to tell me he's a pretty good ballplayer. I know that. But Richie Allen isn't an Oriole."

He said, "There may not be three or four guys in the major leagues with his ability."

I said it again, "Chuck, you can't get to the ballpark twenty minutes before the game and be an Oriole. We don't go for shit like that and you know it."

He said, "I know it. You could do this: Write in his contract that he has to be there at a certain time."

Tanner's a friend of mine, but that's when I lost a lot of respect for him as a manager.

Still, maybe it sounds funny but Tanner could manage an expansion team for me.

And another who could was Preston Gomez. I watched him manage an expansion team at San Diego. He'd tell his players, "Don't take the ballgame home with you. Let me worry about it. If we lose, just look to tomorrow." I thought that was outstanding advice for an expansion ballclub, because you know you're going to lose about 110 times your first year.

Then there's the subject of coaches.

Harry Walker and Charlie Lau kind of invented the position of batting coach, and Walt Hriniak is the modern disciple of their thinking. I tend to feel of their general approach the way someone in baseball once told me about Walker in his heyday: "If you get a guy who's not a power hitter, Harry Walker can do a lot of things with him. But if you've got a power hitter, keep him away from Harry. He'll make him a Punch and Judy hitter."

I liked the approach of the late Ted Kluszewski, who had more of a role than a lot of people thought in keeping those great

Cincinnati bats fine-tuned through the 1970s. Ted told me once, "The best approach for me is not to go to them, because if I do, they won't be as receptive as if I wait and they come to me. When they start struggling, they'll ask me to help. Then I know they'll listen."

Ted could listen, too. The Reds and Orioles didn't get together for a trade for eight years after the Frank Robinson deal—just happened that way, I suppose. But when we did make a deal, it basically sent outfielder Merv Rettenmund and infielder Junior Kennedy from our club for pitcher Ross Grimsley.

Like the Robinson trade eight years before, the deal was made at the winter meetings, and I remember running into Sparky afterward and all he could do was grin. I knew what that grin was saying: "Thanks a hell of a lot. You guys just got the biggest flake in baseball." Ross *was* flaky, but I liked what I saw from him in the National League, and left-handers weren't exactly a commodity. Cincinnati didn't like his long hair. I didn't like it, either, but he won 18 ballgames for us and we won our division. I liked that.

But one day during that season when Grimsley was winning for us, I was watching a Reds game and Kluszewski said, "Can you tell me anything about Rettenmund? I was told the guy was a good hitter, but he is *really* struggling, and I can't figure it out." I said, "Let me tell you what happened with him, Ted. I don't know if it's the reason for his problems right now, but. . ."

Ironically, the story I told him brought that same old name back into play: Frank Robinson. After the 1971 season, when Frank was thirty-six but still a pretty solid player (.281, 28 homers, 99 RBI—about $3-million a year by today's standards), we traded him to the Dodgers. Rettenmund, a hell of a football player at Ball State, had been a solid player for us. He hit .322 in 1970 with 18 home runs; .318 in 1971 with 11 home runs—not too bad. But with Frank gone, Earl called Rettenmund over in spring training and said, "I know you've led our club in hitting two years in a row, but we don't have Frank any more. You're going to have to start pulling the ball. As strong as you are, you ought to hit more home runs."

Now, Rettenmund was the kind of hitter who used the whole field—up the middle, left field, right field. But, oh, man. You can't tell a guy who's not a home run hitter that all of a sudden he's got to start pulling the ball. But all I said to Ted was, "Rettenmund is the kind of guy who if his manager said, 'Swim the Mississippi River,' he would swim the Mississippi River. He'd do anything his manager asked him to do. Two years ago, Earl asked him to start hitting home runs."

Kluszewski said, "That's it. That's my answer." I didn't have to say another word. But it didn't help. Poor Merv stuck around in the majors for six more years but never got his stroke back. His big league career average was .306 before that Robinson trade, and .245 afterward. And the two biggest home run years he had were those with 18 and 11, when he wasn't trying to pull the ball.

13

Nothing Golden
About Rajah

I've heard and read romantic tales of sports' Golden Age, about
how much more glorious baseball was in the 1920s with Ruth
and Gehrig and the 1930s with Dizzy Dean and the Gashouse
Gang and the 1940s with Williams, DiMaggio, Musial and Feller.
I'm sure I'd have enjoyed the game any time, but one brief exposure to one of those greats of the 1920s made me appreciate today's athletes and today's attitudes.

Rogers Hornsby did that for me.

Hornsby was one of those stars who made baseball's Roar-
ing Twenties roar. He won six straight batting championships,
and over the last five (1921-25) of those averaged over .400. Obviously he was a great player.

Bill Veeck was such a romanticist about the game that a
player of Hornsby's ability figured to be one of his heroes.
That's the only reason I can give for Veeck's decision to make
Hornsby the Browns' manager in 1952, which in Veeck-Browns
terms was Year 1 AM, After the Midget—and Year 1 for Jim
Russo, too, but the Midget was a better milestone. Hornsby
was supposed to give us a touch of dignity, I guess, an all-time
great gracing the dugout of a bad baseball team.

Hornsby was introduced to our players at a pre-training minicamp Veeck set up for us in El Centro, California, on February 1 that year, a month before the other major league clubs started training. El Centro is a desert town. February weather was no problem.

Facilities were. Tony Robello, who was our full-time scout on the West Coast and therefore my boss as well as my benefactor, was told to take me with him to El Centro and help him set up the camp. It was all exciting to me. I had been hired just a few months before that. But I learned setting up camp in this particular case meant starting from scratch. Example: we had to drive into San Diego to buy netting so we could build our own batting cage.

When Hornsby arrived, he told Tony and me, "In about a week, I'd like to play an intrasquad game. We're not going to have enough ballplayers here, so maybe you can round some ballplayers up." Tony went out to get some high school and college kids who could play pretty well, and the first man he went to for help was a former minor league pitcher from out there, Nate Moreland, who was still pitching some and knew the local players.

Nate was black. Now, this is five years after Jackie Robinson, and five years after the Browns had their own first black players, so we weren't exactly breaking barriers when we asked Nate to help us round up players. He agreed to do it, and he came out to the ballpark a day or two before we were going to begin. We introduced him, and Hornsby turned to Tony and said, "Now, get me those players—I don't care how good they are. It doesn't make any difference. We just want to put nine guys out there. Round up as many as you can, so we'll be able to play a game.

"But I don't want any niggers around."

Nate was standing right there.

That was the great Rogers Hornsby.

Robello and I were furious. Tony called our director of scouting, Jim McLaughlin, at three in the morning and resigned. McLaughlin calmed him down and told him that Hornsby was an arrogant bigot and would not be around long—which turned out to be the case. I didn't know what to do, but I felt terrible. Tony Robello was my mentor, the man responsible for my being hired by the Browns.

About the only star-quality player we had on our roster was Ned Garver, whose 20-win season with a last-place team had come the season before. He not only was one of the best pitchers in the league but also one of the hardest workers. One day in Burbank, California, it was raining like hell. The pitchers had been doing their running for conditioning, but when it started to pour, they all quit running and went inside—all but Garver. He had a windbreaker on and he stayed out there getting his running in. That's why he was a hell of a pitcher.

He also was traditionally slow about coming around. That first spring under Hornsby, he said ''I hope he lets me get ready my own way. I never look good in spring training. I like to take my time getting ready for opening day.''

Hornsby was old-school: ''He'll get ready like the rest of them.''

So, he pushed him along, Ned came up with a sore arm, and he never was the same again.

That was the great Rogers Hornsby.

His managing career with the Browns lasted until June. Barely fifty games into the season, he was dumped for a former crosstown favorite, Marty Marion.

I did get one more glimpse of Hornsby at work.

The last year we trained in Arizona, 1958, Paul Richards asked me to take a look at a couple of other clubs training in the area with us to see how our young players compared with theirs. One of those was the Cubs, whose established star was their shortstop, Ernie Banks. The Cubs had brought Hornsby in as a batting instructor, and the first thing I noticed when I went to check out the Cubs was that Ernie Banks was the player Hornsby was working with—not the three dozen others who needed some hitting instruction but Banks, who was a born hitter.

That was something I noticed in a lot of specialty coaches:

they'd spend their time with the best, not the needy, on the theory I guess that the expectable results would make them look good.

The only thing that made the Hornsby-Banks case different was what I knew from that day back in El Centro. Apparently Banks' skin color didn't matter so much if those sweet wrists of his could make the great Rogers Hornsby look like a teacher.

I've had baseball people ask me, "After all these years, was there a ballplayer you thought was a superstar type who didn't quite get there?"

The name I mention right away is Ellis Valentine, a big, good-looking outfielder who came up in the Montreal system in the mid-1970s. If ever I saw a ballplayer blessed with all the tools—I mean every one of them, arm, hit, run, throw, speed, power, the whole damn works—it was Valentine.

I'll tell you how good he looked: They brought Valentine and Andre Dawson along at about the same time, and right from the start, Dawson was what he has remained for almost twenty years: a hell of a ballplayer, a leader, to me a superstar.

And as good as Dawson was and is, I think Ellis Valentine had even better tools. The two years they were side-by-side in the Expos' outfield, Valentine slightly outproduced him. But in the long run, there was no contest.

Valentine didn't take care of himself as well as Dawson did. He hung around the big leagues for ten years but had only three productive seasons. He got himself involved with drugs and brought on some of his own troubles.

But he also got hit in the face once with a pretty good fast-ball. I know exactly what he went through, because we had the same thing with Paul Blair, a player I was particularly fond of and proud of because I helped to steal him. I saw him as a young player in the instructional league, when he belonged to the Mets. He looked real good there to me, but for some reason the Mets didn't protect him on their roster, even though they had room. For $12,000, we drafted and acquired a guy who became one of the best defensive centerfielders in the game—and a pretty damned good hitter and leadoff man, too, till that fastball hit him in the face.

Blair had a five-hour operation. He had a broken orbital. They had plastic surgeons, oral surgeons, they were all there. He came out of it with his sight, but he was never the same player again. Earl Weaver eventually started platooning him, using him only against left-handed pitchers. Paul objected, but Earl did him a hell of a favor.

I know courage was never a problem with Paul Blair, and after seeing that experience, I would never, ever be critical of a ballplayer who shows a little shyness at the plate after he has been hit. Until you've been hit in the head by a 90 to 100 mph fastball, you don't know *how* you would act, and I sure don't know how I would.

Dickie Thon is a terrific example of courage in action. Thon was hit in the head by a hell of a fastball. His vision was affected. A very promising career seemed about over. He just wouldn't give up, and he made it back. He's a damned good player again, and one of the guttiest I've ever seen.

Ellis Valentine didn't make it back, but God blessed him with some of the best ability any man ever had.

Adolfo Phillips was another player I thought should have been a hell of a player. He didn't have Valentine's overall ability, but he could do a lot of things. If ever there was a player who was intimidated by a pitcher, it was Phillips. I watched and I couldn't understand it. These guys were sailing pitches under Adolfo's chin, knocking him down, and the Cub pitchers weren't retaliating. I asked Leo Durocher one time, "Leo, I see your ballclub a lot. I see your centerfielder getting knocked down, and knocked down again, and knocked down again, and your pitchers don't do anything about it. Have you mellowed?" Leo said, "My God-damned pitchers are too timid to do anything about it."

I felt sorry for Adolfo. They drove him right out of the league, and nobody retaliated. But there was the difference. How many times was Robinson knocked down? He hung over the plate, and guys like Drysdale—wham! Knocked him on his ass. He'd get up and park one. Poor Adolfo got up and struck out. But, gee, he had a lot of tools.

I just don't think you can have, or at least show, fear and be able to play in the major leagues. I've heard people say, "gutless—that guy doesn't have any guts." Somebody said that at a fall meeting we had one time, when we were all sitting around discussing the farm system, and Paul Richards said, "I don't like to hear that word. Gentlemen, as far as I'm concerned, it takes guts to put the uniform on." And that ended that. Think about it. It does take a certain amount of guts to put a uniform on and go out there and look at a 90-mile an hour fastball. But if a batter showed just a tiny bit of fear, the Drysdales of the game were sharks tasting blood, and that nervous batter was their meat.

Nothing is more exasperating to a scout than a player with outstanding ability who steadfastly refuses to use it. Alex Johnson was an example: strong, fast, good batting eye, good swing—he won one American League batting championship and had a couple of .300 seasons in the other league. And he barely scratched the level of his ability. He never was on our club, and still the way he wasted his talent infuriated me.

At one of the winter meetings, I saw Marvin Miller in the lobby. Marvin was the head of the players' union—I never cared much for him, but I thought he did a hell of a job for the ballplayers. And so did the ballplayers.

This time, I went up to him and said, "Marvin, some of your ballplayers are stealing money."

He looked at me kind of funny and said, "What do you mean?"

I said, "They're stealing money."

He said, "Give me an example."

That was the opening I wanted:

"Alex Johnson. This guy, whenever I see him, almost makes me throw up. He is the biggest dog I ever saw in baseball—no hustle, no attitude, no good. He doesn't want to play. For Christ's sake, he doesn't even run out ground balls."

He said, "Well, maybe there's something wrong with him."

He's defending him!

I said, "People are paying good money to watch him play. This guy is stealing their money."

He came back, "Well, maybe there's something wrong with him."

I said, "Well then why the hell don't you appoint a psychiatrist, I'll talk baseball into appointing a psychiatrist, and we'll find out what the hell is wrong with him.

"But in the meantime, Marvin, he's stealing money."

In 1991, Miller came out with a book: *A Whole Different Ball Game—the Sport and Business of Baseball*. I laughed out loud when I read *Sports Illustrated* reviewer Ron Fimrite's comment that Miller blasted owners, agents, sportswriters and "even—now that, through him, they've gotten what they want and are acting complacent about it—ungrateful players."

That's what I was talking about, Marvin. Welcome aboard.

Not all the baseball head cases were as cantankerous as Alex Johnson.

The early Orioles had a dandy in Jackie Brandt. God really gave him some ability. He could run, he could hit, he could throw the ball. And he was flaky.

He was playing for us when Richards managed the club. One day he went to the plate with the bases loaded, took three straight strikes, and sat down. Never swung the bat. It never so much as twitched.

Back in the dugout, Richards looked at him and said, "Jackie, were you guessing up there?"

"Yeah," he said. "I was guessing inside and they were outside."

Now, a guy may say he was looking for a fastball and got a breaking ball, or vice versa, but not inside-outside. And certainly not with the bases loaded.

Richards was beside himself.

"We've got to find a place to send this guy."

(A postscript: For a few years, Jackie actually managed in the minor leagues for somebody. It wasn't us.)

The hardest thrower I believe I ever saw never made it to the major leagues, for which batters can be grateful, because I know he was the wildest pitcher I ever saw.

Steve Dalkowski created his own legends in baseball in the 1960s, so much so that old-time scouts still talk about him.

He was a left-hander—not very big, 5-10 and 160. He was eighteen when we signed him, and his first professional season was a tipoff of what was to come.

He was 1-8 for Kingsport, in Rookie League. That's bad.

He gave up 22 hits in 62 innings. That's remarkably good, better than any major league pitcher ever has done.

He struck out 121 in those 62 innings, which is an average of nearly 18 per nine-inning game—far above the best season of Nolan Ryan or Sandy Koufax.

He walked even more—129, or almost 19 per nine-inning game, which is why a man who averaged pitching a three-hitter had an earned run average of 8.13.

By then, he surely had our attention. Everyone in our system knew about the wild left-hander who threw flame.

I'm not at all sure he could spell flame, though. He was dumb, awfully dumb. You could see that in a hurry. And he turned out to be an alcoholic, on the cheap stuff, wine.

One night when I went to see him pitch, I noticed that he and the catcher were discussing the plate umpire, whom they didn't particularly like. I overheard enough to figure out that Dalkowski was going to throw a high fastball and the catcher would stay down instead of coming up to catch it. The obvious idea was to hit the umpire, with a ball flying somewhere around 100 miles an hour.

I said, "Wait a minute. You pull shit like that and you're going to go home tomorrow. Maybe tonight."

A little stunt like that could have been fatal. Dalkowski hit one guy unintentionally and just tore his ear off. He accidentally nailed an umpire, and shattered his mask. I know it's physically impossible, but it seemed like the last third of the way to the plate, his fastball just took off.

When I was a kid, I saw Bob Feller. He belongs on any fastball list. So, of course, did Nolan Ryan, Sandy Koufax and someone you might not remember, Jim Maloney of the 1960s Reds. The 1990 World Champion Reds had a candidate, too: relief pitcher Rob Dibble. Ryne Duren and Goose Gossage were other relief pitchers with exceptional fastballs.

Ryne started out as one of our guys, with the St. Louis Browns. He wore glasses as thick as Coke bottles, and it wasn't an act. The guy just couldn't see. When he still was with us, someone hid his glasses when he was sleeping once, and when he couldn't find them, he wouldn't get out of bed. Now, I'm not saying there wasn't an act to the Duren who eventually made it big with the Yankees. Every time he came in to a game, at least one of his warmup pitches would sail clear over the catcher and splat against the backstop with a sound that rocked the stadium—and probably was noticed by the batter due up. Stories were that twice he hit batters in the on-deck circle, more of the act that certainly worked to keep batters loose. The word didn't get around, in his peak years, that Ryne was fighting an alcoholism problem, too. The prospect of a blind drunk on the mound throwing as hard as he did and as wildly as he did on his best days would really have made for what Roy Campanella used to call the ol' jelly leg. All I know is the eyesight part wasn't fiction. Ryne couldn't see.

But I don't think he or Dibble or Ryan or Feller or the best of the acknowledged hard throwers could have matched Steve Dalkowski's fastball.

Dalkowski put up numbers that no one ever approached, a lot of them negative. He hung on for nine seasons, just on promise, twice rising as high as Triple A.

Somewhere along the line, we should have called him up—say, for an inning or two against one of those Yankee teams we chased. I'd have paid my way in to see how brave those guys were stepping up against him.

It truly is a shame that an arm like that never did throw a major league pitch. I called him dumb. We weren't a bit smarter, in some ways.

I remember I was on the road in 1959 and Dalkowski was pitching for Earl Weaver at Aberdeen. During a phone conversation, Harry Dalton mentioned that Steve had pitched the night before...pretty well...threw two-hundred-eighty pitches.

I said, "Threw HOW many?"

Harry repeated the number and broke it down into how many strikes and how many balls. I said, "For Christ's sake, Harry, haven't you sent a memo to our minor league managers setting a limit on how many pitches our kids can throw?" Evidently, it had never dawned on him, and it never dawned on Weaver, who sat right in the dugout that night as Dalkowski's manager and watched it happen.

A few years later, Dalkowski seemed to be getting the pieces together, but he came up with a bad arm. As with Billy Martin and those A's pitchers he burned out, and Paul Richards and the young pitchers of ours that I felt he abused, overuse may have contributed to the breaking point in Dalkowski's fragile career. Time makes it obvious that his arm problems can't really be traced to that two-hundred-eighty-pitch game, but I will say there's no way Dalkowski or anybody should be allowed to throw that many pitches—certainly not a power pitcher.

14

Can't Fire the Owner

The people who squandered the savings and loans billions must have gotten their start in a baseball front office, or been grooming themselves for getting there. There are twenty-six teams in major league baseball, and twenty-six theories on how money should be spent in operating the franchise. The game has become a millionaires' toy, so the normal orderly process of working with a budget toward a respectable profit margin is totally distorted. Some of today's owners don't care how much money they lose if they win a championship—not on the theory that it takes money to make money but that it's all a big yacht race and I want the glory of getting across the line first, whatever the cost.

And some owners don't care how much their team wins if the profits are maximized. I'm not sure which is worse for the game. The free spender sounds better to that team's fans, but inevitably the person throwing the money around sees himself or herself as the captain of the ship and steers it with the skill of the guy who ran the Exxon Valdez. The profiteer never seems to catch on that the truly big reward goes to the team that strikes a good balance of investing in farm systems and building a team of good men and good players, fairly paid. Even that's not enough. There's also the matter of paying some attention to the fans who show up at the ballpark, and—first things last—finding a "baseball man" to direct the whole thing. That's the step that most of today's owners can't or won't take. If they're paying for the hand, they want to play the cards—no matter how lousy they are at knowing when to hold 'em and when to fold 'em.

I used the term "baseball man" when I meant someone, anyone, who knew the game and had some common sense. It doesn't always go with intelligence. Gen. Elwood "Pete" Quesada was obviously a very bright man, but when he bought the Washington Senators, one of the first things he told his scouts was: "Gentlemen, the most exciting play in baseball is not the home run, it's the triple. I want you to sign players who will hit triples."

Now, he could have said, "In our big ballpark, I'm not as much interested in pure power hitters as I am in stocking our team with contact hitters who use the whole field and have enough speed to stretch singles into doubles and doubles into triples." That's a little different from sending a guy out to sign triples hitters.

It was comforting, in sort of a reverse chauvinist way, to learn in 1990 that male baseball owners didn't have a monopoly on silliness. Marge Schott of the Reds couldn't even look good winning a World Series.

Now, Marge is not exactly the matron saint of scouts. She's the one who cut severely into her organization's scouting budget and phrased her reason in one of the great baseball questions of all times: "Why should I pay all that money to scouts? All they do is sit around and watch games."

She said that while in the process of nickel-and-diming her way through a pruning that eliminated some outstanding scouts. She lost her farm director, Larry Doughty, who became general manager of the Pirates. She lost another one, Greg Riddoch, who became manager of the Padres.

It would have been more devastating personally when the

Reds stunned the A's in four games if the fine hand of scouts had not been so evident in the championship club. Eric Davis, Barry Larkin, Chris Sabo, Paul O'Neill, Joe Oliver, Tom Browning and Rob Dibble all came right up through the system, signed by guys who just sat around and watched some ballgames. And that four-game sweep of Oakland didn't just happen. Jimmy Stewart did a wonderful job of scouting the A's, one of the best ballclubs to come along for a while.

If Mrs. Schott felt vindicated by that sweep, it didn't take long for her to foul it up.

Only George Steinbrenner could conceivably have botched that great October triumph into a public relations disaster as quickly as Marge did. The Series ended in Oakland, and one of the Reds' heroes, outfielder Eric Davis, missed the celebration at the ballpark because he had injured himself pretty severely—with internal hemorrhaging—diving for a line drive early in the fourth game. Davis was admitted to an Oakland hospital and not just for overnight observation. There was genuine concern for his welfare.

After a few days, understandably wanting to be with his teammates enjoying the heady hours when victory was still fresh, Davis got permission from attending physicians to fly back to Cincinnati—if the trip was by chartered jet, allowing constant attention by doctors making the trip with him. The bill came out to $15,000.

And the Reds refused to pay it.

This was the man whose first-inning home run off Dave Stewart in the opening game of the Series had about the same kind of effect on the 1990 Reds that Frank Robinson's homer had for our 1966 Orioles, instantly infusing confidence in first-time Series participants who might have had some secret doubts. Yes, he was being paid one of baseball's enormous salaries, but the man got hurt making a legitimate, even exceptional, effort on the playing field, not in a bar someplace.

Several days later, the Reds agreed to pay the airplane bill. Not nearly so many heard about that as heard that the brand new world championship team was playing El Cheapo with one of its stars. The decision made in embarrassment wouldn't have cost one more cent if made in exultation right away, as it should have been. It was the start of a downward swirl for Davis as a Red, leading to an off-year for him in 1991 and his trade—to the Dodgers, primarily for a good-looking right-handed pitcher, Tim Belcher, in the off-season. I couldn't help remembering that line from my high school books: "Those who cannot remember the past are condemned to repeat it." Davis was about to turn thirty; remember Frank Robinson was "an old thirty" when the Reds dealt him? A really good right-handed pitcher was the allure—both times.

The chintziness about getting Davis home after the Series in 1990 and the team's troubled 1991 season may have been just a tiny illustration of what Mrs. Schott ultimately will learn. In baseball, bad decisions don't always take their toll immediately. When she gutted her scouting staff, costing her some key people in management as well as the unfortunate scouts she sacked, she started a quality-reduction process that may not be evident for five years or more. But it will show up.

The situation reminded me of when Phillip K. Wrigley, the chewing gum guy, owned the Chicago Cubs in the 1950s and 1960s. He sat in on the Cubs' organization meeting one winter, and to impress him the player personnel people gave him one glowing report after another on young players they had in their system. Obviously, the intent was to make themselves look great and maybe sweeten their paychecks.

They reckoned without ownership mentality. "I can't tell you how happy I am to hear all this," Mr. Wrigley told them. "I guess that means we don't need to spend any money this year on signing new players." And he wasn't kidding. The budget was all but eliminated for a year, and cut back for several, because it's difficult to add lines to any budget, once they're removed.

It took a few years, but that air bubble in the blood vessels ultimately worked it way to the heart of the club. The Cubs lost games on the field for years after they lost Mr. Wrigley's money, all because of some attempted owner manipulation that back-fired.

And then you can have a man like Gene Autry, who has just plain been robbed.

Gene has done everything I have said an owner should do. He has put up the money to finance a first-rate organization—he probably has spent more money on his club since taking over the California Angels in 1961 than any other owner in baseball.

And he still has not won.

My definition of winning is getting to the World Series. You may or may not win there, but getting there is the goal. The Angels have won a couple of division titles, but they never have taken Autry to the World Series. He has put up the money, turned baseball decisions over to "baseball men," and he has been screwed. The Cowboy deserved better—and maybe Whitey Herzog, the latest man he put in charge, can deliver it.

They're a diverse breed, owners. I got to know many of them well, and even admired some of them. Let me introduce you to a few.

Charlie Finley

Charles O. Finley was a character of the game I really enjoyed.

Good for baseball? Bad for baseball? I'm not a good judge, because he was good for Jim Russo—a good friend.

I got to know him over the years, but in his final seasons, I knew him better because our general manager then was Hank Peters, who had worked for him and been fired. Whenever anything came up where we had to deal with Charlie, Hank would always say—and I mean always: "You talk to him. I can't stand the SOB."

So I would drop by his Chicago office—he ran the A's from there, with an 800 number on his telephone line. And every time I ever went in that office, there were Internal Revenue Service people going through things. One time right in the middle of everything was a huge sack of peanuts, sent to him by Jimmy Carter. The IRS people went through those, too.

Charlie took over the A's in Kansas City. He inherited a bad club and worse farm system, but he went to work with a pretty good scouting staff and started building. That was just before the draft began, and the first player taken in the first draft was outfielder Rick Monday of Arizona State, by Charlie Finley. He got Sal Bando and Gene Tenace in the same draft. The next year, he drafted second, behind the Mets. They took a catcher named Steve Chilcott—a California kid they said later was recommended by Casey Stengel, who had retired by then and was living in Glendale. Charlie took advantage of the opening they gave him by picking outfielder Reggie Jackson of Arizona State. He had a good position in those early drafts, but he also made shrewd picks. In those days, he listened to his scouts, and his scouts did an excellent job.

One by one Charlie built the team that won three straight World Series in the 1970s. Catfish Hunter, Joe Rudi, Rollie Fingers, Campy Campaneris (Charlie always insisted the best player he ever had was Campaneris), Vida Blue—every one of them came just like Monday, Jackson, Bando and Tenace, right out of the farm system. They were good teams, good enough that sometimes they won playing to spite Charlie.

He could be as hard to work for as George Steinbrenner on George's worst day. Charlie actually sat in Chicago and made up his team's lineup, then called it out to Oakland. Every day. He took a guy out of the mail room, made him a vice president, and his job was to take Charlie's call and give the lineup he dictated to the manager.

One night, it was almost game time and they hadn't had a phone call from Charlie. The manager—I think it was Jim Marshall—was desperate: "Christ, I've got to turn in a lineup to the umpire." He's writing one down real fast, standing at home plate—and here comes the vice president, running like hell, carrying a sheet of paper. The game went on.

In building the A's, Charlie put together a good scouting staff and used it well. As the years passed, though, he got himself into a position where he felt he couldn't trust anybody, and that's a sorry situation to be in.

When the A's were still in Kansas City and Hank Peters was the farm director, Felix Delgado, his Latin American scout, signed a ballplayer on Christmas day. Charlie by then was personally going over every expense account, he was that convinced everybody was sticking it to him. When he came to the Christmas signing, he called Peters in and said, "What the hell is this—so much food, so much travel December 25?" Hank told him who was signed and confirmed, "I gave the OK." Charlie didn't believe him: "Don't give me that bullshit. *Nobody* works on Christmas Day."

And that was with the receipts in his hand. I understood a little of why Hank turned him over to me and wanted nothing whatsoever to do with him after getting out of there. How could you work in conditions like that?

I don't know what ever became of that Christmas day signee, but I do know Rollie Fingers was signed by the A's on Christmas Eve. I wonder if Charlie questioned that one.

As he worked himself more and more into that paranoia, he brought me more into his counsel on baseball matters. I never saw it as a conflict of interest to give him advice on moves he might be considering. I happened to know that half the general managers in baseball were helping him. Each had his own motivations. I just felt, "I'm not going to say no to the guy. That couldn't hurt the Orioles." And it didn't.

We did do a little business. We sent Don Baylor and Mike Torrez and a young pitcher, Paul Mitchell, to Charlie for Reggie Jackson, Ken Holtzman and a minor league player. Our guys, when we called them in the office in spring training in Miami and told them, cried. His didn't.

My involvement with him came after he had built his team and during the period when it was coming apart, partly because of his own stubbornness and partly because the commissioner of baseball, Bowie Kuhn, was about as objective on Charlie Finley as Ron Luciano was on Earl Weaver. Kuhn put a knife in Charlie when he voided the sale or trade of all his players who wound up leaving him for free agency—without remuneration. Desperate owners have sold prized players for years. Lord knows we did it with the Browns. Kuhn stopped Finley under that "best interests of baseball" bullshit that amounted to a one-man vendetta—which, in truth, had been waged both ways. Charlie hated Kuhn, too.

Charlie created a lot of his problems. If he were to level with someone today, he would have to admit that he did some screwy things. The whole free agency problem with Catfish Hunter started because Hunter just wanted some of his paycheck channeled in another direction, to an insurance policy. Charlie was an insurance man, for Christ's sake. He let his own obstinance enter into situations that wound up hurting not just Charlie Finley but baseball in general.

But some of his ideas weren't so bad—night World Series games, flashier uniforms. I never thought he'd get away with the white shoes, because baseball has had a long tradition of denying the pitcher any kind of distraction that might take a hitter's attention away—flapping sleeves, jewelry, anything. And here they allowed Charlie's pitchers to raise that white shoe right in a batter's face when he was trying to pick up a white baseball coming out of there.

He also wanted the ball to be orange. That didn't sell. And he wanted to give walks for three balls, not four. I was totally against that. Some young pitchers with a tendency toward wildness never would have escaped the minor leagues.

But that was Charlie, always thinking about ways to improve his team and/or the game, not always for his own benefit. It became sad. Here was a guy who used to enjoy life and truly enjoy baseball, and now he felt like everybody was out to get him. But the man did put some good clubs on the field. Very good. You win three world championships in a row, that's not luck.

Charlie and his wife divorced before Charlie and Hank Peters did. She nailed him. She got their big farm along the Indiana toll road outside LaPorte, the one where Charlie, when he was a new club owner and proud as hell about it, put the A's logo on the barn roof for every traveler to see. Last I heard, that logo was still there, but Charlie was long gone from the premises.

The divorce did not make Charlie's life monastic. I never, ever saw him without a beautiful girl. He had a Chicago apartment right on Lake Michigan—beautiful. And his harem seemed to be crazy about him.

Charlie and I and one of his girls went out to dinner one night, and I was nailed with the check. I said to myself, "I'm going to have some fun." Charlie got up and went to the kitchen, and she said, "I really like him. Charlie is such a nice guy." I said, "Has Charlie bought you a car yet?" She said, "No!... why?" I said, "Oh, I don't know, I just know he bought his other two girl friends cars." She said, "No!"

I lied a little. But I figured she probably nailed him pretty good later.

When I retired from the Orioles in 1987, my kids had a retirement party for me in Florida, during spring training. Charlie sent me a telegram from Chicago: "I'm sorry I couldn't make your party, but you made me what I am today."

I think it was a compliment.

Ted Turner

Ted Turner, the Atlanta TV mogul who got into baseball by buying the Braves, was another guy always with some woman other than his wife—always very good-looking, almost as good-looking as Charlie Finley would have around him.

One year, the winter meetings were in Hawaii. I was in the hotel lobby, ready to go to dinner, standing with Tom Marr, one of our play-by-play announcers, when Turner walked up, escorted as always by a lovely, lovely girl that he obviously was trying to impress.

He said, "Would you guys be willing to talk about Jim Palmer?"

Now, this was when Palmer was at his absolute peak, but I

knew he had probably picked Jim's name to drop because he was one of the few players the girl might have heard of.

But I went along with him: "Ted, you know how it is in baseball. You're always willing to talk, about anybody. I'm sure we would be, if we found an opportunity to improve ourselves."

He said, "Well, I just want you to know that I've got a lot of interest in him. We'd be willing to give you value for value received."

I said, "The only thing I can tell you is Palmer does have the right to veto trades and he has always indicated that he would only go with a winning ballclub, not with a loser."

His eyes got big. He's trying to impress his girl friend and I'm telling him he's got a horseshit ballclub.

He said, "Well, we're starting to win..."

But he had had it. He walked off, and if he didn't say it I know he was thinking, "That no-good son of a bitch."

I honestly wasn't trying to show him up. I just gave it to him as straight as I could. But Tom Marr thought it was funny as hell and told everybody in our organization what happened.

Turner survived it well. In 1991, his Braves played in the World Series, his network (CNN) taught the big ones how to cover a war and *Time* named him Man of the Year.

Maybe now he could get Jim Palmer.

George Steinbrenner

George Steinbrenner was Charlie Finley with New York as his amplifier—all of Finley's bombast and ego and paranoia but oh so much louder because of New York.

The years from his acquisition of the club to his ouster from baseball by Commissioner Fay Vincent in the summer of 1990 amounted to one long run on Broadway for the biggest show in town: George.

He read himself into everything that happened or was said in baseball, which accounted for one of my first involvements with him.

I'm not even sure what year it was, maybe 1980, but I was in spring training at St. Petersburg looking at the various clubs that train in central Florida. I was just chatting with Joe Durso, a *New York Times* writer whom I've known for a long time, and he said: "Tell me about the success of the Orioles. Every year you guys are either right there or you win it."

I told him I thought it was a combination of a lot of things, but one of the real important things that might usually get lost in trying to explain something like that was the role of our owner, Jerry Hoffberger.

I said, "Joe, he doesn't interfere with us, and that's important in baseball. You've got to be able to go out and do your job. You've got to be able to do what you have to do without interference from ownership. We know we've got his support. We also know that if we don't do a decent job, he'll fire us, and that's the way it should be.

"But he doesn't interfere with us. He's told us: 'I hired you people because I think you know what you're supposed to do and that's it.' "

Joe wrote the story. I didn't mention Steinbrenner. I can't say he never crossed my mind while I was talking about that subject, because he was such an obvious symbol of the total opposite of the situation I was describing, but evidently Steinbrenner felt: "This is an insinuation."

No it wasn't. It was an answer, to a direct question about the reasons for our success. There were a lot of things; that was just one of them. But if your hands are tied, you can't do the kind of job you want to do. And I don't think I or Joe Durso had to tell anybody that if you work for Steinbrenner, your hands are tied.

He never said anything to me. He ignored me, but I did get feedback that he was upset. George is a great competitor, and I admire him for that. He wants to win. Obviously he felt his way was the right way to be successful. Maybe it was, but not for me. I can't feel afraid to act. I've got to do it the way I think I should. If I do it the wrong way, fire me. You're justified.

The Steinbrenner stories became legend. I've heard a lot of

them, from friends who managed for him or played for him or scouted for him. I don't even know who the manager was—it probably happened, in some form, to every one of the dozen or so different guys he had as manager—but one day the Yankees had the bases loaded with two outs in the first inning. A fairly weak hitter popped up, and George made it a point to walk to the back side of the dugout, lean over and yell, "Didn't you ever hear of a God-damn pinch hitter, you son of a bitch?"

When the ax came down on George, I'll admit to some feelings of sadness, because I know the guy had his good side, and he did try. But at the same time, I was happy for baseball, because it indicated at last we have a commissioner with guts. The owners, after all, are the guys who pick the commissioner, and decide if he stays or goes. It was one thing for Bowie Kuhn to take on a maverick in Charlie Finley. It's another for Fay Vincent to thumb out the owner of the New York Yankees.

It will be interesting to see how that translates to voting support when Vincent comes up for contract renewal. It should be encouraged as the very kind of independent firmness needed to show players that the commissioner is a true administrator of baseball, not a tool of the owners because they hire him. In this era of enormous financial figures, I don't know if that kind of stature ever can be gained by a commissioner in any sport, but it would be invaluable in times of threatened strikes of lockouts or other player-owner strifes if some element of mutual trust could be extended to the commissioner. To me, Fay Vincent took a big step toward earning that trust by daring to act against George Steinbrenner.

Edward Bennett Williams

I think the main reason George Steinbrenner took offense to my comment about Orioles owners was that he was totally unequipped to understand what I was talking about: how it feels to try to operate from the other end of the owner-employee relationship. That was the only end I ever occupied, and I was sincere when I said how much it helped me in my work to be employed by the kind of owners I was always fortunate to have with Baltimore.

One of those was Edward Bennett Williams, who in many ways was a bigger and more familiar household name before he ever got to the Orioles' ownership than was Brooks or Frank Robinson, Earl Weaver or anybody else in baseball.

Williams was a brilliant trial lawyer, an adviser to presidents, a political kingmaker—hell, the man represented countries. And, God rest his soul, he was probably the closest thing we had to a Steinbrenner in that he had a problem keeping his earnest interest in the ballclub and the players from turning into meddling. But there was still a huge difference between Edward Bennett Williams and George Steinbrenner in intrusion.

Williams bought our club just after the 1979 World Series. Not long into the 1980 season, I could see things had started to change. Some of the ballplayers were being criticized in the newspaper—not viciously, but Jerry Hoffberger would never criticize a ballplayer to the media.

And Williams thought nothing of calling a player when the ballclub was on the road and giving him a pep talk. Maybe that works in personnel-relations seminars, but when a ballplayer is struggling, the last thing he wants is a phone call from the owner giving him a rah-rah pep talk. It was usually a negative, not a positive.

But having a legal mind like Mr. Williams' around was a treat.

During one of our off-season baseball meetings, we discussed something we were planning to do with one of our players and he said, "I'd hate to have to defend that."

I hadn't heard that kind of terminology around a baseball table before, but it certainly was a sign of the times.

When the subject of competing financially for free agents came up, some of us were for staying out of it and focusing our attention on our own farm system. Mr Williams warned us that if we did that we could get nailed for collusion.

That upset me. I said, "Wait a minute. Let me change this

from a hypothetical situation to a real one. We brought up an out-fielder named Mike Young this year, and Mike had a good rookie year—not great but solid and it looks like he's blossoming just about the way we, and he, had hoped.

"Now, in the off-season, here's this free agent available, he plays the same position Mike Young plays—are we supposed to tell Mike Young, 'Mike, we're sorry as hell. We know you had a good year this year, but you're going to have to go back to Rochester and we're going to have to go after this free agent because we don't want to get nailed for collusion.' "

I said, "Mr. Williams, your farm system costs you several million dollars a year. And now we can't use it? Why have a farm system?"

He looked at me like, "Russo, you don't understand law."

It turned out he was right—on how difficult it would be for baseball to defend itself against a collusion finding, and about my understanding of law.

There was collusion. There's no doubt about it. I still have a problem with bringing a kid through your farm system to the point where he's ready to try—maybe not succeed, but try. And somebody else says you should spend money to sign somebody with better credentials, but no loyalty at all to your organization and no sense of belonging. I don't think owners should be allowed to get together and decide how much or how little they will spend, as—in effect—apparently was done, but I damned well think any owner ought to be free to say free agency is not the route he wants to take in building his team.

But legally? In the words of the late and great Mr. Williams, "I'd hate to have to defend that."

Brad Corbett

There are a couple of owners I almost worked for—in the years after the Orioles' great success put a spotlight on a lot of us.

When Brad Corbett owned the Texas club, I got to know him pretty well. He ran that club—ran it into the ground with his terrible deals.

He wanted to make me his general manager. I turned him down. I said, "You've got Eddie Robinson."

He said, "I'll make Eddie the president but I want you running the ballclub."

I said, "Brad, I have no desire to come over here. In the first place, I'm happy where I am. And secondly, you know you're going to run this show. You don't need me."

I'm sure there were guys who would have jumped at it, but I didn't want to have a job like that with puppet strings I could see before I even got there. If they want you to be the general manager, you've got to have sole responsibility and make the moves, or you're general manager in name only.

The other team was the Cardinals.

When the Cardinals let Bing Devine go as general manager, club owner Gussie Busch's No. 1 man, Lou Susman, said he wanted me to take the job.

He said, "There are two guys that I'm committed to talk to, and I'm going to New York right now to talk to them. But you're the guy I want."

A lot of thoughts ran through my mind quickly. At the time, I didn't know manager Whitey Herzog particularly well, but he had played for us in Baltimore so there was some familiarity, and I had enough admiration and respect for him as a manager that I thought, "I could get along with Whitey."

I hadn't even had much time to mull the possibilities over before I was at the St. Louis airport making a trip one day, and I see Whitey Herzog and Joe McDonald practically running through the airport.

They went straight out to talk to Mr. Busch, who made the decision to hire McDonald right there—he didn't even wait for Susman. And just that quickly, my flame of interest with the Cardinals died.

I look back at it now and I think it might have been for the best. It wasn't exactly like the Corbett situation in Texas, but the Cardinal operation had its own problems built in—a lot of interference in the ballclub's operation by brewery people Gussie appointed, plus some from Gussie's own attorney, the man who wanted to hire me: Susman, who apparently didn't have as much clout with Gussie as he thought he had.

Jerry Hoffberger

I have reserved for last on my owners' list my favorite: the fellow Steinbrenner thought I was comparing him to, which I would never do. No owner I ever dealt with, certainly not George Steinbrenner, compared with Jerry Hoffberger.

What a wonderful human being. Every day in the newspapers or on television you see where a player and the front office are battling, and the player will say some version of "I can't wait to get out of this town."

That didn't happen with the Orioles and Jerry Hoffberger. Jerry loved his players, and they had respect for him. One of the reasons he got out of baseball was the first players' strike. He could not believe the players would do that to management, and he was obviously heartbroken when some of our players elected to strike—I think he felt he had done so much for them, looking after their welfare.

When Brooks Robinson ran into financial problems, Jerry immediately got in touch with Ron Shapiro, who at the time was an agent for most of our players and was very, very good at looking after their investments. He put Robinson in Shapiro's hands and got all that straightened out, because he cared about Brooks Robinson the person, not just Brooks Robinson the Hall of Fame ballplayer.

He cared very deeply about a catcher named Dick Brown, too, as all of us did.

Dick might have been our catcher on the 1966 championship team, but in spring training that year, our team physician, Dr. Leonard Wallenstein, gave the players their physicals. Most of the physicals go rather routinely, but when he used that little light to look into Brown's eyes, he didn't say anything for a minute. Then the doctor said, "Dick, I think I'm going to send you back to Baltimore for some tests."

He had a brain tumor. There was surgery, radiation treatments, all of the desperate and expensive things that are done in those tragic cases. The Dick Brown battle lasted almost four years, but he died in 1970. No one knew all the nice things Jerry Hoffberger did for Dick and his family through that period, but everyone on our club knew he was doing everything he could. Our players deeply appreciated that kind of feeling from the man in charge—and that obviously came through to the people who paid to watch the Orioles. One of the lasting memories I have of the days I spent in Cooperstown for Jim Palmer's induction into the Hall of Fame is of the number of fans who nostalgically talked of those years and mentioned how different things were: the atmosphere around the club, which, whether they knew it or not, was in large part created by the man at the top.

I can assure you it wasn't only our players who felt our club owner was someone special. I have a houseful of baseball treasures and souvenirs, files full of reports and letters. And I have one letter that I cherish above all, dated March 3, 1987, just after my retirement from the Orioles and when I was going to be honored by the Baltimore chapter of the Baseball Writers of America.

Dear Jim:

There comes a time when each of us has to retire. I've done it twice but I must say without much success either time. There is always so much to do and that's the way it will be for you, as well. Hopefully, you will play lots of golf and go to ball games just for the fun of it. And there will be much more, too. All the people who look up to you will want to gather around to hear your fabulous baseball stories.

Don't forget to tell them how you helped a real "rookie" put together an organization which has supplied more top-level baseball people to the game than any other club...how you led a scouting staff in a way which gave the "rookie" manager the substance and courage to make fantastic deals...and how you took pride in the success of every kid you nurtured through the tough years in the minors and the even tougher ones in the big leagues . . . and how you agonized over every lad who had the talent but got messed up in some way.

Tell all who will listen, and so many will, that the year was 1965 and that I am the "rookie." You tell them that and I'll tell them why we called you "super." Lots of people will think it was because you are a scout "par excellence" and they would be partially right. I always used that name because you are a "super" guy, one who always told it straight but with great sensitivity—a person this "rookie" could always depend on.

Be well, "Super." Come see us. We will always be in the phone book, and the welcome mat will be there forever for the likes of you.

Sincerely,

Jerry (signed)

15

The Brewery Money

Let me show you how baseball spending works, using as an example one of the most successful operations in the game: the St. Louis Cardinals.

Begin by understanding what the Cardinals have represented to me throughout my own professional career: money, in huge, overpowering amounts.

When I joined the St. Louis Browns organization, the deck wasn't really stacked. The Cardinals always had more money to work with than we did, but, hell, so did a lot of corner gas stations. Pitifully small amounts were monumental barriers to us. We could have had Yogi Berra, a St. Louis boy, but we lost him to the Yankees because we couldn't come up with $500.

But, with the DeWitt brothers, and later Bill Veeck, we had strapped but shrewd baseball men running our operation, and we at least could dream of a chance—even in a town that had been Cardinal-loving since the 1920s. Because of Branch Rickey—and Grover Cleveland Alexander and Frankie Frisch and Dizzy Dean and Pepper Martin and Marty Marion and Enos Slaughter and the greatest of them all, Stan Musial—the Cardinals were a hell of a franchise, let alone a tough rival to share a town and a ballpark with.

But the Browns did meet them in the 1944 World Series, and our organization was able to function with the idea that a little extra work could overcome the dollar handicap and maybe come up with the next Stan Musial and win it all.

All of that changed the day the beer money bought the Cardinals and squeezed out Bill Veeck. Everyone knew we had to go, including the other American League club owners, who saw the situation as their chance to get rid of maverick Veeck and conditioned permission for the franchise shift on finding new owners.

I loved Veeck and hated to see him lose out, but I held no real grudge against the Cardinals because their push changed our franchise's whole way of life. In Baltimore, we found money of our own to operate with, and fan following that was all ours— not 85 percent the other guy's. The great Oriole teams of the 1960s and 1970s might never have happened in Brown uniforms.

So maybe it was an instinctive act of unacknowledged appreciation that prompted me to align myself with the Cardinals— once.

A big reason I did it was Whitey Herzog. I really admired the job the guy did as the Cardinals' manager. No one has a bigger effect on the way the game is played than he does. I used to join our club four or five times during the season, and when we went into Kansas City, the same thing always happened: they would force us into more mistakes then I've ever seen the Orioles make, just by taking that extra base and throwing all that aggressiveness at us that they call "Whiteyball." I told him one time, "In the first place, you can do more with one or two runs than any manager I've ever seen. And secondly, you can force the other ballclub into more damned mistakes than anybody I've known. I wish to hell I could do my job as well as you do yours." He had a big smile on his face.

We haven't always smiled at each other.

In 1982, just before spring training, the Cardinals got Ozzie Smith from San Diego, and right away Ozzie was asking for more money—$300,000 more than he was making with San Diego. Baseball has an established procedure for arbitration of salary differences between clubs and veteran players, but this was different—at spring training time, much later than the usual off-season arbitration period.

I knew it was happening, but I hadn't thought much about it one way or the other until Hank Peters, our general manager at the time, got a call from Joe McDonald, the Cardinals' general manager, McDonald asked if he could use me in the arbitration case as an expert witness. Hank said it was up to me, the Orioles had no objections.

He asked, and I jumped at the chance, because the whole arbitration procedure had irritated me for a long time. It wasn't my money involved, but dammit, it bothered me when undeserving guys kept using the system to get more money than they were worth. My accent there is on undeserving. The deserving guys with big contracts—and there are many—*are* the game. Arbitration, which baseball brought on itself with dictatorial behavior by owners as long as they had the power to be dictators, I think unfairly extends the reward for the good players' excellence to the marginal or even poor players who can build some bridge of common accomplishment with guys they'd never even be mentioned with in trade discussions.

It happens because of how the whole thing works. When a case goes to arbitration, someone—not necessarily a baseball expert; in fact, some of those arbitrators have been dumb as hell about the game—is designated to hear the club's case for the salary offer it is making, and the player's case for what he's asking, and pick one or the other figure, not a compromise between the two but one or the other.

I've been told in one arbitration case, the guy making the decision interrupted the testimony to ask, "What do you mean, save? What is a save?" Can you believe baseball—players and owners—jointly agreed to set up a situation where major salary decisions were made by people that ignorant about the game?

That wasn't the case in the Smith case. The arbitrator was

Tom Roberts, and he is acknowledged to be one of the best—smart as hell.

Joe McDonald told me, "We would like to have your help. Give us any advice that you possibly can. We're not too sure we can win this case, and if we lose it, it's going to cost us $300,000."

I'm already in Florida for spring training, but I had that feeling about making a stand against unwarranted salaries and said, "OK, I'll go along with it. Let me have a few days to decide what plan we should use, how we should go about it, and then I'll let you know." Lou Susman, Gussie Busch's personal attorney, called me and thanked me for agreeing to help. He said, "Now, the minute you're ready to talk to our lawyers we'll have them fly down to St. Petersburg and sit down with you." About three days later, I tell them I think I've got a plan that will get the job done. They said, "Fine."

They flew down two lawyers from Susman's office, Dan Ball and Mike O'Keefe. I told them, "I think I've got a plan that can get the job done. We've got a guy on our ballclub who is known throughout baseball as perhaps the finest fielding shortstop in the game. His name is Mark Belanger." They had never heard of him. The further we went the more I realized these guys knew surprisingly little about baseball. I couldn't believe it—that Susman's law office would stick the Cardinals for two round-trip air tickets to Florida, for two full lawyer's days and whatever in hell that cost, and send two guys who barely could carry on a baseball conversation.

But I went on. "Here's what I think will really win this case. We're paying Belanger $169,800, and Ozzie Smith is asking $750,000. I will testify that I see every player in the major leagues and I've seen every shortstop in baseball, and I am prepared to compare every shortstop in baseball with Ozzie Smith—all of them, in all phases of the game. But we will start with Belanger, whom we all consider one of the premier fielding shortstops in baseball, and Ozzie, who hadn't hit much better than Belanger, is asking for almost five times as much as he's making. There can't be that much difference."

They got their pencils out. I went down a list of every shortstop in the major leagues, even the utility guys. Beside each name, I would make my comparison of that player with Ozzie—"same," meaning the player was the same as Ozzie in total value, in my opinion; "better," if I thought Ozzie was better; "not as good," if I preferred someone over Ozzie—who, remember, wasn't "The Wizard of Oz" then. He was coming off three seasons in San Diego where nobody had ever seen him and he had hit .211, .230 and .221.

I mentioned that batting part, because it's a factor in evaluating a good-field, no-hit player. I told them, "When you get into a close game, Whitey might have to hit for Ozzie, so you don't even get the full nine defensive innings out of him then. I want you to be sure to ask me about that when I'm testifying." And I said, "Guys, I don't see how we can lose this case."

They told me, "The Cardinals are going to compensate you for this." I said, "Right now, I'm interested in how we're going to win this case." That was a mistake. I didn't say, "All right, let's talk about money right now." I was flattered that they asked me, but I threw everything into the case. I just felt, "Dammit, give it everything you've got. Make the preparation so good that you win the case."

In the meantime, I was living just a couple of doors from Whitey and his family in spring training. I had a condo in Isla Del Sol and they had one three units away. Whitey kept telling me, "You're the one I wanted on this." Joe McDonald would say, "I'm the one who wanted you to do this." Susman is giving me the same bullshit. I said to myself, "I'm not going to worry about pay. I think the world's largest brewery will be fair."

The arbitration procedure was in San Diego. Ozzie is there with his wife. I had sat with him once in a coffee shop in Philadelphia, and under these conditions in San Diego, Ozzie was the same: real gentlemanly, a real nice person.

They called us in one at a time. Juan Bonilla, who played second base for San Diego, told Roberts, "I know how good he is because I play beside him."

Then it came my turn. I have to hold my hand up and get

sworn in, the whole thing. Of course I was going to tell the truth, but a lot of it was going to be my judgment.

So the lawyer asks me questions:

"Do you know Mark Belanger?"

Yes, he plays shortstop for the Baltimore Orioles.

"How is he regarded in baseball?"

We consider him perhaps the best-fielding shortstop in baseball.

"*Field*ing shortstop?"

Yes, he's had only one good year offensively, but with our ballclub we can compensate for that.

"How much does Belanger make a year?"

$169,800.

"And you say he's the best-fielding shortstop."

Yes, I think he's the best.

They asked me to compare him with other shortstops, and I went down my list. Ozzie was sitting there with his wife. Once in a while, when I gave an answer, he would wince, smile, and shake his head like "You don't think I'm better than he is?" Another time he would shake his head to say pretty emphatically, "You're wrong. You're wrong." The first thing I had said on the stand, though, was directly to his wife: "Mrs. Smith, I want to say one thing to you. I don't know your husband real well, but I have met him. I think you're married to one of the nicest people in baseball."

We won the case hands down.

A couple of weeks later, there's a check in the mail from the Cardinals, signed by Joe McDonald and someone else.

For $1,000.

I said to myself, "Well, they can stick this thing right up their ass."

I called Joe and let him know I felt greatly underpaid. I said, "I know we never discussed money. Maybe that's my fault. I'll take the blame for it. I thought we had more important things to do, to put this case together and go out and win the damned thing, because baseball has been hurt enough by these guys asking for millions of dollars."

He said, "This is what they told me to send you, but if you're not happy with it...."

I said, "No, Joe, I'm not. I'll send it back to you."

I get another check in the mail for $1,500.

I called and said, "Joe, I don't even want to mess around with this." He didn't either. He said, "Why don't you call Lou Susman? I'm just doing what they told me to do."

So I called Lou. Only a few years before that, Lou had wanted to hire me as general manager, right before Whitey got Joe McDonald. He said, "Well, how much do you want?" I said, "I don't even know. You people came to *me*, you asked Baltimore's permission, you wanted me. I was more than happy to help you because by doing it I thought I helped every club in baseball, ours included."

He said, "Well, we think what we gave you is fair, Jim. That's the best we can do."

I said to myself, "I'll give Herzog a call. He said he was the one who wanted me." I called him one morning and said, "Whitey, you *know* this is a piece of shit."

He said, "What do you think it's worth? What do you have in mind?"

I said, "Well you saved $300,000. It ought to be worth 6 percent."

He said, "You mean $18,000?"

I said, "Yeah, in that neighborhood."

He said, "Well, I'll be a son of a bitch. We'd have won that God-damned case anyway. Fuck you!" And he hung up.

Susman called back and said, "Why don't you come over to the office, Jim, and we'll sit down and talk about this." I went over to his law office, and he said, "Jim, what's the problem?" I said, "No big problem, Lou. You people had a lot of people in baseball to choose from and you asked me. I just think $1,500 is a little bit insulting." He said, "Are you gonna sue us?" I said, "I haven't said anything about suing anybody, for Christ's sake." O'Keefe was sitting there and Susman said, "O'Keefe tells me a couple of times in conversation with you they asked you what you wanted." They didn't ask me that at all. They said, "The Cardinals will compensate you." And that thought I had when they said it came back to me: "The world's largest brewery will be fair."

Susman said, "Jim, that's the best we can do. If you want to sue us, do it."

I went back home and talked to my kids about it, and they said, "Aw, the hell with it, Dad. Just go ahead and cash the thing." I really shouldn't have. The money wasn't that important to me. (Or to the Cardinals, apparently. Three years after they connived to cut corners on him with my testimony, the Cardinals made Ozzie Smith their first $2-million-a-year player. Figure that one out. Then, when he got to $3 million and was worth every penny, they went on a penny-pinching movement and looked around to find someone who would take him off their hands—when he was hitting .300 and playing almost as well as ever in the field.)

The Cardinals eventually did a flip-flop on Whitey Herzog, too—and, I am absolutely convinced, lied a little.

When Whitey "resigned" as Cardinals manager in 1990, ostensibly out of frustration because he couldn't get the club to win, I think he in truth was fired by the brewery boys, who don't like the corporate image soiled by identification with last place.

My evidence?

In accepting Whitey's "resignation," the club announced that he would be paid for the duration of his contract.

Ask the man who saved them $300,000 and was told to take half-a-penny on the dollar and be happy, *that* bunch from that brewery wouldn't have paid Whitey an extra dime if they hadn't fired him.

The world's largest brewery has some cheap bastards making decisions.

16

The View from Over the Hill

I was retired and pretty well cushioned from any responsibility when the Orioles—my Orioles—became the joke of baseball, the St. Louis Browns days all over again. We were the franchise with the best record in all of baseball from 1960 on, right up through that year. But not even the old Browns did what the 1988 Orioles did. They lost their first twenty-one games.

It tore my heart out, and I wasn't there. I'd turn on the network news—not the sports but the world news—and another Orioles loss was such a big event it was included. The Dickens line, "the best of times...the worst of times," came back to me. All those years that were the best of times, how had we become the worst so soon?

That's a part of baseball that is tricky. Things can come apart almost overnight, but for the most part baseball operates with a long lead time. I firmly believe the downfall of the Orioles began a dozen years before that, when Jerry Hoffberger moved Frank Cashen from baseball operations to the brewery he owned (National) and turned the Orioles over to Hank Peters.

That was 1976, and a lot of good things happened for the

Orioles after that, including the key trade with the Yankees for Scott McGregor, Tippy Martinez and Rick Dempsey that led to our 1979 American League pennant and the 1983 world championship. Obviously, Hank did some things right.

But the thing about him I said to myself so many times was, "He's just not a heavyweight." I'll give you a personal example why:

When I was working for Jim McLaughlin, Lee MacPhail or Frank Cashen, at contract time they would call me and say, "I want you to fly into Baltimore so we can sit down and talk about your contract." That made me feel pretty good. I'd fly in, spend a couple of days, sit down and talk about the contract, shake hands and go. Or, I might be in for our club's fall meeting and we'd take care of it then, before I went home.

It didn't happen that way with Hank. I'd be in Baltimore, the subject of a contract would never come up, then I'd fly home and the contract would be there, in the mail. Or it might come in two days later. And I would be thinking, "I was right there, for Christ's sake. Why didn't he have the balls to sit down and talk about it?"

Hank didn't seem able to meet you face to face. To me, there's something missing in his makeup that I think costs an organization camaraderie, if nothing else. (Harry Dalton didn't do it that way, but he would find every way in God's creation to tell you you did a bad job so he could beat you down a hundred dollars.)

Hank also had a habit of promising something and failing to carry it out. Lee May and Al Bumbry were two of the most popular Orioles, and when their playing days were over, Hank Peters publicly said he would take them on as coaches. It never happened; Lee went to work for Kansas City, although Hank told me he offered Lee as much as the Royals did. I asked Lee why he took their offer instead of ours. Simple answer: Hank, intentionally or not, misinformed me; Kansas City made a far better offer.

Even that was better than how Al Bumbry was treated. I was at a banquet where Al was honored, and the reaction of the

Baltimore people to him then obviously impressed Hank Peters. He said after the dinner that Al would be offered a job with the organization. I asked Al about it later. The Orioles never did make him an offer. Last I saw he had survived another managerial change and was still coaching first base for Boston.

So I guess I was lucky I got a contract at all from Hank Peters. He came in, inheriting the most successful organization in baseball, and made a lot of changes.

Hank brought Tom Giordano in as our director of scouting. He immediately started firing longtime, loyal Oriole scouts and hiring guys who were his friends, guys he and Hank had at Kansas City.

A primary example was our Florida scout, Joe McIlvane, who has gone on to big things—he did such a great job as vice president of player personnel for the Mets in the late 1980s that the Padres hired him as their general manager.

Giordano fired him.

Why? His explanation to me was, ''Jim, he missed a ballplayer down in Florida—a hell of a player. McIlvane said he couldn't play. I'm gonna replace him.'' The scout doesn't exist who hasn't missed some players, but he fired McIlvane and replaced him with the former Giants pitcher, Jack Sanford, who was with him in Kansas City.

Sorry. I don't understand the mentality of a person who would come in and start doing all this to an organization that has been so successful.

I hope McIlvane can appreciate the pleasure I got from one very private victory.

Giordano kept telling me what a great connoisseur of food he was. He isn't a bad cook himself. I'll give him that. But he told me how well he knew Italian food and said, ''I'll take you to some of the best places.'' Check my name. Finding good Italian food was not an area in which I thought I needed a hell of a lot of help.

But one year the baseball convention was in Toronto, and Giordano set it up for twelve of us to go out to dinner. He'd called the restaurant and critiqued everything: style of food, the way they cook, everything. "Just great," he said.

We went there, ordered, and the meal was disappointing. Giordano admitted it. He said, "Jeezus Christ, I don't understand this. I called. This place was recommended. I don't understand it."

I said, "Tom, I've never been here, but I knew an hour ago we weren't in a real good restaurant—when they handed each of us a plastic menu like they have at an all-night diner. As great a connoisseur as you are...did you ever see a good restaurant with a plastic menu?"

All he could say was, "By God, you're right."

Ironically, that all-time-record losing streak opening the 1988 season represented the first twenty-one games in the regime of general manager Roland Hemond, brought in by Edward Bennett Williams after he fired Hank Peters—and Tom Giordano—at the end of the 1987 season.

I'm sure Mr. Williams didn't think about it, but his pick achieved a neat bit of baseball symmetry. You'll remember that the baseball lords denied Bill Veeck the chance to go to Baltimore with his St. Louis Browns, forcing him to sell to local interests.

When Veeck last surfaced with the White Sox, his right-hand man was Roland Hemond, for whom Veeck had enormous respect.

A year after that 0-21 start, Hemond had put together an overachieving ballclub that stayed in contention for the division championship until the final week of the 1989 season. Bill Veeck would have been proud of the way he did it: cheaply.

I wasn't so much proud as relieved, that maybe the great times weren't back but at least the blushing over Baltimore had ended so quickly.

In retirement I could think about something I never did when active—my own personal, scout's-view all-star team. Let's try it.

You scout players for offense, except for shortstop. It's great if your shortstop can hit, icing on the cake. But I want a glove there. The hell with the bat.

That's why the three best shortstops I've ever seen were Looie Aparicio, Mark Belanger and Ozzie Smith. Aparicio and Smith actually had some pretty good years with the bat. Belanger had one good year but mostly poor ones—with the bat, never with the glove. He should have been better as a hitter. He had the speed to help himself with bunts or drag bunts, but he wouldn't do that. In the field, they're three about whom I will use that word great. There's no other word.

And the one from that three that I'll put on my personal all-star team? I'll take Looie. I felt so strongly about him that I lobbied with some writer friends of mine who were hesitant about giving him their vote for the Hall of Fame. I asked them, "Are you not going to vote for him because he didn't hit the ball out of the ballpark? He did everything else." He got in, and he belongs there. And I suspect Ozzie Smith will, too, for the same reasons. Belanger never will, but they were the three greatest I ever saw. But I'm keeping my mind open on Cal Ripken. It's not *totally* a defensive position.

I'll go primarily with offense on the rest of my team, although the guys I have in mind won a lot of gold gloves, too.

Catching: No contest. When you look at 650 players every year, you can have a tough time settling on one: "If I pick this guy I'm not doing justice to another guy." But if you're starting a franchise, and you have your choice of one ballplayer, from any position, it's got to be Johnny Bench. He was durable, had power, could hit, throw and receive.

First base: Willie McCovey. There were some very good ones, but day-in and day-out, over a considerable period of time, Willie was dominating, and not at all bad with the glove.

Second base: That's tough. I've seen some good ones, including Ryne Sandberg today—a real good player. But I'll take Joe Morgan. With him I get everything: hitting, power, speed, base-stealing, defense. Plus leadership—he was the National League MVP in both 1975 and 1976. He made the double play very well. He and Luis Aparicio would have been a terrific combination.

Third base: Look, I really liked Mike Schmidt. And George Brett was outstanding. But, Brooks Robinson starts on MY team. When you commit just 263 errors in 9,165 chances and win sixteen gold gloves, you have a hell of a chance to make my ballclub. I've always felt the first order of business in any sport is to keep the other team from scoring, and that was routine for Brooks. He was also a clutch hitter; my club is full of those. The only weak category for him is speed, but my team is covered there. Some said his arm wasn't very strong. All I know is I never—*never*—saw anyone reach first base because Brooks didn't have enough on his throw. He almost redefined the term "quick release."

Outfield: Ted Williams, Joe DiMaggio and Stan Musial came before my scouting, which leaves me with just Willie Mays, Mickey Mantle and—of course—Frank Robinson. Mays did everything, a complete player who also was one of the most colorful players ever. Mantle, as a switch-hitter, helps to balance my team, but that's a minor consideration compared to the power and speed he brings. And Frank Robinson? I'll get, and fully understand, arguments for Henry Aaron over Frank. I like Aaron personally, and as a player—obviously. He was (here's the word) great. But I feel Robinson's leadership with the Orioles was more profound than was Aaron's with Milwaukee or Atlanta.

Pitching: I'd take Sandy Koufax as my left-hander, unquestionably—although Whitey Ford and Warren Spahn were pretty good, and for a three- or four-year period, Mike Cuellar was remarkably good. But Koufax was the best left-handed pitcher in modern-day baseball, although an arthritic left elbow (which might have been reparable with today's surgery) ended his career at thirty-one. He was so good he meant 15,000 extra fans whenever he pitched. He'll help pay my team's bills. For my right-hander, I couldn't leave Bob Gibson off. Unless it was for Catfish Hunter. Or for a personal favorite: Jim Palmer. But, much as I love Jim Palmer, I'd have to say Gibson. I saw five no-hitters in my career, but the most impressive, most overpowering pitching performance I ever saw was Bob Gibson's 17-strikeout game against Detroit in the 1968 World Series. He was a good hitter and fielder, too. He's one pitcher who probably could have played in the majors at another position.

Relief pitcher: Among right-handers, I loved Rollie Fingers. Great slider—just awful tough. Goose Gossage at his peak and Dennis Eckersley from today's group rate with anybody. But I actually felt sorry for hitters when Bruce Sutter, in his best years, came in, so Sutter is my pick. His split-finger fastball embarrassed batters. He was another whose career was shortened by arm problems, but the splitter makes him my right-handed choice, because the splitter makes it almost irrelevant whether the batter is right- or left-handed. Among left-handers, Sparky Lyle is my choice—originally signed by the Orioles and drafted away by Boston. His screwball made him almost as effective against right-handed hitters as left, and he was remarkably durable. Baseball has had many good left-handed relief pitchers, including the Orioles' own Tippy Martinez, but that ability to go out there almost every day—the key to his Cy Young Award in 1977—makes Lyle my choice, even if Earl didn't have room for him on that damned 1970 All-Star team.

I mentioned the Fingers slider: That one pitch, relatively new to the game, is the main reason I don't think we'll ever see another .400 hitter.

The slider has neutralized a lot of good hitters. It has become the pitch that makes a .270 hitter out of a .300 hitter. It's an outstanding pitch.

Maybe the best I've ever seen at throwing it was Milt Pappas, the key man in our Frank Robinson trade. I thought at the time he was pitching his slider was the best in the big leagues, and now that I look back, and I've seen all the pitchers ever since, it's still as good as I've seen—hard, short, quick.

In the last few years the slider has gotten bigger, to where it's hard to tell a slider from a curve ball. Pappas had the old-fashioned slider—the speed of the fastball with a late, quick break. Not big, eight to ten inches. Devastating.

Ferguson Jenkins got to Cooperstown with a combination of a great slider and even better control. Watching Jenkins in his prime throw pitches to Randy Hundley with the Cubs was like watching a game of pitch and catch. Hundley set his glove behind the black on the outside of the plate and Jenkins threw a slider there. Nobody did it better.

Carlton Willey had a very good slider. And Catfish Hunter. Bob Gibson's may have been the hardest. Larry Dierker had one of the best. And Bob Purkey, Lee Stange, Dick Hall—God, there were some great sliders.

And Vachel Perkins, believe it or not, gets on my list, too. We didn't know anything about the slider then. Vachel called it a sailer. But it was a good one.

We used to have a lot of sore arms when the slider first came into vogue. Later, George Bamberger was able to teach it so it didn't create elbow problems. Under Bamberger our sore arms just went out the window. (Of course, the tonsils were gone by then.)

Almost equally devastating to the prospect for ever seeing another .400 hitter was the emergence of the split-finger fastball. The key man in that was Roger Craig, as manager of the San Francisco Giants, and I think it says at least as much about Roger that he did so much with the pitch although he didn't have anything to do with inventing it.

When he was pitching coach at Detroit for Sparky Anderson, I mentioned to Roger one day, "Your pitchers as a group, as far as I'm concerned and I see them all, have the best split-finger fastballs in baseball. What's behind that?"

At the time, the very best at throwing it was the Cubs' relief pitcher, Bruce Sutter. Craig told me he called Sutter one day in the off-season and asked if he could fly to Sutter's home and sit down and talk to him for a couple of days about the split-finger— how he threw it, when, just everything he could find out. That's what Craig did, and he came away with secrets that paid huge dividends for him ever after.

If any coach deserves credit for developing the pitch, it's Freddie Martin, who was an outstanding pitching coach in the Cubs' organization when Sutter was coming along.

The split-finger is thrown with exactly the same motion as the fastball. It comes in and suddenly drops. It has almost the speed of the fastball, but the action at the end makes it a killer. It just falls off a table.

It doesn't seem to take the toll on arms that the slider does, although the slider doesn't have to. George Bamberger showed us that.

17

Manager of the Years

Baseball gave me so very, very much over my thirty-five year career, and in truth it's still giving. It was my great luck to end my active years just when baseball and cable television were taking each other to new levels of national attention.

I would have missed the game a lot more, I'm sure, if I hadn't had Cubs telecasts and Braves telecasts and the last couple of years White Sox telecasts cabled right into my home daily, and if ESPN hadn't come along with a depth and consistency of coverage that in some ways keeps me better abreast of all that's going on in the game than when I was in the middle of it.

It's special to me because I turn on the TV and I see friends. Not all of them are in the dugouts. I've mentioned the job Steve Stone does with the Cubs. Another pitcher, Don Sutton, is part of what I consider the best team of announcers in the game—the one Ted Turner put together at Atlanta. I think Skip Caray is the best in the whole business—analytical but light and cheerful about it; damned witty but not to the point of ridicule; familiar with the game as only years of exposure to players and situations and personalities can make someone. All those years of growing up in ballparks around his dad, Harry, have made him a delight to listen to.

Sutton was always one of my favorites. He had so very much success, because of a combination of talent and intelligence and the good fortune of playing with strong Dodger teams, that it's unfair to him for me to tell of a day when he was neither successful nor—in my judgment—smart. In 1973, the Dodgers were running away with the National League West, eleven games ahead of the Reds when they played a Sunday double-header July 1 in Cincinnati. The Reds were stumbling, and Los Angeles was about to push them twelve back in the opener when an obscure back-up catcher, Hal King, hit a two-out, two-strike, three-run pinch-homer off Sutton in the ninth for a 4-3 win. The Reds went on to sweep the double-header, and win the division. I saw the double-header, and that night at the hotel where the Dodgers and I were staying, I ran into Sutton, who even then was a friend of mine.

He said, "Well, you saw it. What did I do wrong?"

I sure wouldn't have gone up to him and volunteered my opinion, but he asked, so I told him. "For Christ's sake, Don, you're too good to lose like that. You've got a good fastball, a good curve, a good slider, a good change-up. Now you're messing around with a screwball, and that's the pitch you throw to a guy in a position to beat you. You're one of the smartest pitchers in baseball. If you're going to get beat, you can't get beat with your fifth-best pitch."

He looked at me for a second and said, "By God, you're right." We're still friends.

Baseball and I are, too. I have to laugh at people who talk of it as a dying sport. Strikes were going to kill it. The free-agent system was going to kill it. Obscenely high player salaries, high ticket prices, saturation coverage on TV, its slow pace and three-hour games—each of those things, and certainly all of them together, would surely kill it. It doesn't fit TV screens, or TV demographics, or today's lifestyle—it's a dying game, I kept hearing.

Then I picked up the paper at the end of the 1991 season

and saw that 56 million people paid their way into the ballparks. That's better than 2 million per club. OK, so Toronto is an anomaly with its 4 million. Take that out and it's 52 million for twenty-five teams, still 2 million-plus on the average. And it's not four or five teams distorting the average. Virtually every team in both leagues—certainly every team that has made even a hint of sincerely competing for a championship—is above 2 million or near it.

And that wasn't always the case. As recently as 1974, when the A's had one of the most colorful and most successful teams in history, the last of three straight World Series champions drew 845,000, and the average for the whole American League was just 1.1 million.

I loved the flashbacks all through the summer of 1991 about the summer of '41, when Joe DiMaggio had his 56-game hitting streak and Ted Williams hit .406. In all of it there was the hint that baseball was richer then, more attractive to the masses. But, Williams and the Red Sox that year sold 718,497 tickets. DiMaggio and the World Champion Yankees drew 964,722.

It also was the fortieth anniversary year of the Bobby Thomson playoff homer that beat the Dodgers. Counting the three-game playoffs, the Dodgers that year drew 1.28 million, the Giants 1.06 million.

It was the thirtieth anniversary year of Roger Maris' 61-homer season. Mickey Mantle had 54 that year, too; the 1961 Yankees were one of the greatest teams in baseball history, and certainly one of the most entertaining. That glorious Yankee team drew 1.7 million; a lousy one in 1990 drew 2.0 million.

This is dying?

In 1991, the White Sox moved into a new Comiskey Park. A beautiful place. A ballpark, not one of those football-baseball dishes with artificial grass. They drew 2.8 million, a Chicago record.

Nice as it is, I think the one opening up in Baltimore this spring is better. I loved Memorial Stadium—partly for the memories but also because it was a pretty good ballpark. I can't tell you how I look forward to my first visit to Orioles Park at Camden Yards. I'd love to be there opening day. It's brand new, ultra-nice, and tradition-based, which is kind of the way I feel about every baseball game I see: traditional, but new.

One thing those attendance figures tell me is that the fan at the park isn't upset about how long a game takes. Sportswriters and TV people don't like long games because they're there every day. The average fan is there maybe once, twice, possibly five times all year. They rush-rush-rush every day of their life. They're at the ballgame to savor, not to dash in and dash out. Baseball is not a time-clock game.

And it is not a dying game—in the stands or on the field. The athletes playing the game today are the best, ever. They don't have the best attitudes, but they're the best athletes. I marvel nightly at the plays I see them make. I wince sometimes, too, at the fundamental mistakes I see. If some of these guys would ever learn to play the game, they'd really be good.

For all that I cherish from my thirty-five years in the game, I regret some of the price.

My career cost me some things I can't make up: those priceless hours at home watching, and helping, my own children grow from tots to teen-agers to adults. Mine was a small price compared to what it might have been, because I was blessed with a wife who handled the dual job of Dad and Mother when-ever she had to, which is why in retirement I can look at all five of our kids with pride in what they are, not the remorse of won-dering how I could have helped them.

Betty was the Russo family's Manager of the Year. Every year.

I remember only one time she showed even a little bit of ir-ritation with the demands of my job, and I didn't blame her that time. I was feeling a little sorry for myself, let alone for her.

In December 1962, we had a decision to make on a young outfielder: Dave Nicholson. He was one of those big, strong kids who always looked like the next Babe Ruth to Paul Richards. In the spring of 1958, they flew me in to St. Louis to look at him. He had good power, but I really wasn't too high on him. He had an awful problem with contact. The Cubs had an outfielder named Bill Nicholson through the World War II years and beyond, and they called him "Swish." He never struck out as many as 100 times in his sixteen big league seasons. Compared to Dave, he was a contact hitter.

But Richards was crazy about him. We overpowered him with money—$105,000 and two brand new Pontiac automobiles, one for his dad and one for him. Paul always had an in, or an angle. The scout who signed Nicholson, Del Wilber, was a Pontiac salesman in the off-season, so Paul cut a little off the corner there. Still, the edict went out right after that: no more car-giving.

We brought Dave up briefly in 1960, sent him all the way back to C ball at Aberdeen in 1961, then had him back up the last half of the 1962 season. He hit .186 and .173 in those two chances, with almost three times as many strikeouts (131) as hits (51, 14 of them homers).

The homers he hit were exciting. The man did have power, there was no doubt about that. And he was a nice kid. Everybody was pulling for him.

We had played him in almost 100 games that second time up, and the club decided to send him to winter ball in Nicaragua. Then they told me to go down there and watch him, to decide whether we should hold onto him or put him in a deal.

The whole idea seemed dumb to me. We had just looked at him for three months. Now they wanted me to evaluate him under maybe the worst conditions in baseball. This isn't Puerto Rico or Venezuela, this is Nicaragua and the ballpark is just horrible. The stadium—Estadio Somoza, for the dictator in power at the time—had poor lights, complicated by neon advertising signs in the hitting background.

I flew to Managua and when I got there, Nicholson was ready to go home, completely discouraged. He was 0-for-27. His wife and kids were with him, and his kids were sick. He had hurt an ankle, and the local doctor that the Managua club sent him to checked out his ankle by putting a stethoscope to it. Dave said he listened intently, then told him he had arthritis. He was twenty-three at the time.

I sat down with him, told him being there was good for his baseball future, and he should stick it out.

A day or two later, in the rental car he got just to go from the hotel to the ballpark and back, he had an accident. The following day, I saw his name in headlines in the local, Spanish-language paper, and I asked a fellow to translate it for me. The headline said:

"Nicholson Gets His First Hit—a Car."

A couple of nights later, on a radio interview at the ballpark, the first question I was asked was "What the hell's wrong with Nicholson?"

I did my best to defend him. The truth was the Latin pitchers were throwing him a lot of off-speed pitches, because that's the way they pitch. And there was the language barrier— the poor guy was having a rough time. But I said, "You know, he has been injured. And these lights—the natives can play under lights like this, they're used to it, but he's accustomed to better lights. And you've got all these neon signs out there—like that one on the left-field line, 'Lanica Airlines.' How can a right-hand hitter follow the ball with that sign right in his face?"

Lanica happened to be the national airline, owned by the Somoza family. I wasn't aware of that, but it didn't make any difference to me. It apparently did to Somoza. Two days later, some government officials came to the hotel and suggested that I not be so critical about the ballpark and conditions, and that maybe everyone would be a little happier if I made my stay as short as possible. They were suggesting that I leave, and I suggested to them that I was on assignment, and I would stay as long as I damned well needed to. The whole operation was rotten. One of the teams in the league was sponsored by the government. When it played poorly, the paychecks were held up for a few days to get a message across.

I didn't really have to stay very long. I had seen enough. A month later, we packed Nicholson with Hoyt Wilhelm, Pete Ward and Ron Hansen in a deal that brought us Luis Aparicio and Al Smith from the White Sox, who liked the other three but really were excited about the power potential Nicholson offered—if he could just be straightened out. I thought, "Good luck. Give me Looie any day." It was one of the many key moves that ultimately led to our era at the top.

Just as I was getting ready to fly home from Managua, though, Baltimore called. They asked me to go to Panama to see the Caribbean World Series—for all the champions in winter ball in Central and South America and Puerto Rico. Two of our best young players, Dave Johnson and Boog Powell, were on one of the teams, so I understood what they were doing.

Betty didn't. When I called her and told her my plans had been changed and I was going to Panama, she didn't try to hide the fact that she was upset. "I suppose you won't be home for Christmas," she said. I said yes, I would be home for Christmas, but I had to go to Panama.

Then I got to Panama and wished I had listened to Betty. The Panamanians were marching against the United States in the streets, the issue at the moment a demand that the Panama flag be flown alongside the U.S. flag in the Canal Zone. I came in oblivious to it all and checked in at a nice hotel in Panama City. I wasn't there long before the hotel people called my room and said, "Mr. Russo, there could be problems. You might be better off moving somewhere in the Canal Zone." Which I did.

At the stadium, I got the scare of my life, and it didn't have anything to do with the demonstrators. The night of the championship game, as part of the hoopla, they shot off fireworks from the top of one dugout. Bill Veeck would have loved it, but he would have done it with better marksmen. These guys meant to shoot the fireworks straight up but accidentally sent them straight out onto the field—with our team on the field, ready to play. All of a sudden I was looking out at an entire infield engulfed in smoke, with the right side of our future infield—Dave Johnson and Boog Powell—somewhere out there in it. All I could think was, "Oh, my God, there goes our infield, in one puff of smoke."

They survived, I saw the games, and I got home for Christmas—enormously relieved.

The routine Betty and I had worked out for my road trips

usually worked a lot better than that. I called her every day—or at least, every other day. And I'd make up an itinerary three weeks in advance, so she always knew where I'd be.

In the summer of 1980, we were going to be playing Toronto, so I was in Texas on a Saturday, watching Toronto against the Rangers. My plans were to stay through Sunday, then fly from there to New York to pick up the Yankees for advance work on another series.

But, I had seen Toronto quite a bit by then, so I said to myself, "I think I'll go home tomorrow and go to New York on Monday from St. Louis." I called that night and told Betty I was changing plans: "I'll be home tomorrow. The plane gets in around 11:45." She always took me to the airport and picked me up.

I was standing at the curb at the St. Louis airport with my bags when I saw our car drive up—with my son Ron and one of my daughters, Jennifer, in it.

They gave me the news that Betty had died of a heart attack that morning.

I wasn't there, when she might have needed me most. But the doctors have told me it wouldn't have made any difference if I had been. She had hardening of the arteries, and she apparently went instantly. Ron said he got up that morning to make himself breakfast and Betty was on the couch, reading the paper. He went upstairs, came back down later, and she was gone. She had even talked about that: that's the way she wanted to go.

I won't say she disliked baseball, but she didn't pretend to know anything about it. She knew the Orioles were in the American League. She went to several World Series, whenever we were in it. And I took her to spring training several times.

I remember the contingent of wives we had at that first Series for us, in Los Angeles in 1966. Most of them paid as much attention to Cary Grant sitting near them as they did to the Dodgers and the Orioles. I'm sure Betty did.

She was at Cincinnati when we beat the Big Red Machine in 1970, and in Pittsburgh when the Pirates beat us in 1971. She saw them all. But she didn't know much about the game, and I certainly didn't force it on her.

I think any woman married to a man in baseball—scout, manager, player, coach—has to be very strong, because of the demands. Baseball wives deserve a hell of a lot more credit than they get.

I traveled seven months out of the year, almost constantly. There was always the baseball winter meetings. And while the Nicaragua-Panama trip was one of a kind, I did see a lot of winter ball—Puerto Rico, Venezuela, the Florida instructional leagues.

I was gone when three of our five children were born.

Nancy was the fifth one. Dalton Jones was a hotshot shortstop in Baton Rouge, Louisiana, and the club told me, "You have to see him because all the ballclubs are looking." It was May, and Betty was due. I told her, "I don't want to go down there. You're ready to deliver." She said, "Don't worry about me. Go on and see the ballplayer. I'll be all right." I talked to her doctor and he said, "Jim, it could be any time—a few days, a week. I'll call you. Betty isn't the type who needs a lot of attention."

So I flew down there, went to the ballpark, and Ted Williams was there—the Red Sox had asked him to go see Dalton Jones. I looked at Dalton, and, sure I liked him—you had to. But I determined quickly in my mind that he wasn't a shortstop, which is what we really needed. I always felt shortstops were born—if you can play shortstop, you can probably play another position, but if you aren't born to play shortstop, you can't be taught. Offhand, I can think of only one exception: Bill Russell of the Dodgers.

So, I had dinner, went to my room—and about 10:30 that night the phone rang. It was Betty. She said, "Guess where I am. I'm in the hospital, and you had a little girl at 7:30 this evening."

I was home for the first two, Ron and Susan. The other three, I wasn't—not for Cliff, Nancy or Jennifer. I was in spring training when Jennifer was born. Three out of five...

It did not bother Betty. She was a strong person. She never felt she had to have attention.

And I wasn't there when I always will wish that I had been, just on the longshot chance that I could have helped her.

I did a lot of thinking while I was home that time. I looked around at my kids, all grown, and realized how lucky I was because we never had any trouble with any of them. Amazing.

The ballclub told me, ''Take as much time as you want.'' But I knew I would be better off if I got right back, rather than stay around home and mope.

So I did. As a matter of fact, I called Earl Weaver from the funeral home and gave him the rundown on Toronto.

After all, I expected our players to play when it hurt a little. Or a lot.

That's baseball.

Index